Michael Bash

EVOLUTION
BY GOD

Discover the explosive secret of God's real name. Learn how it bridges the gap between science and religion and why it was kept hidden for 3,000 years!

THIS BOOK IS PUBLISHED BY
Ink & Quill Publishers

A Division of
Imagined Interprises, Inc.

For more information please visit
www.evolutionbygod.com

Sr. Content Editor - Roberta Edgar
Content Editor - Maxwell Alexander Drake
Proof Editor - Lorraine Stalians

Published in the United States by Michael Bash
9075 W. Diablo Dr.
3rd Floor
Las Vegas, NV 89148

www.evolutionbygod.com

Published by Ink & Quill Publishers
ISBN: 978-1-936525-95-9 (Paperback)
First Edition: October 2012
Printed in the United States of America

Library of Congress Copyright TXu 1-813-187

This book is dedicated to my late parents, Meir and Ahuvah Bash, and to my grandfather, Dov Ber Bash;

To my mother, who taught me how to love God and to "love your neighbor;"

To my father, who taught me how to worship God and make mammon;

To my grandfather, a chemist and a Talmudic scholar, who taught me how to cherish the Talmud and admire science;

To my ninth-generation grandfather, Rabbi Schneur Zalman (the "Rebbe"), author of the Tanya, whose spirit has followed me all the days of my life.

ACKNOWLEDGMENTS

Writing a book is a team effort. I am taking this opportunity to thank those members of my extraordinary support system and creative team without whose commitment and inspiration this book would not have seen the printed page.

My sincere thanks to:

Rabbi Harold Kushner, bestselling author of *Why Bad Things Happen to Good People*, for providing me with the benefit of his time, talent, and wisdom in a comprehensive critique of this book.

Notable scientists Victor Stenger (fellow alumnus of the New Jersey Institute of Technology) and Gerald L. Schroeder, for their professional encouragement.

Bestselling authors, Richard Dawkins, the late Christopher Hitchens, and the collective atheist/author community (in addition to nameless numbers of religious fundamentalist writers and preachers), for providing me with endless fodder for the material contained herein.

Polina Chebotareva, for infusing me with ongoing inspiration and confidence to complete this worthy project.

Roberta Edgar, writer and editor, for helping to crystallize my thoughts, enrich my narrative, and elevate my material to lofty new heights.

Maxwell Alexander Drake, author and publisher, for so beautifully formatting and publishing this book.

Terry Barone, graphic designer, for his contribution of strikingly relevant images.

And a special thanks to God for making everything possible, including the transformation of a businessman like me into a published author.

TABLE OF CONTENTS

FOREWORD

Hello,

My name is Maxwell Alexander Drake, and I am an award-winning science fiction/fantasy author, graphic novelist, and playwright. You may be wondering why someone like me would be attached to a project like this. I asked myself the same when it discovered me. I say that this project discovered me because that is the only way to describe it.

I was brought in to help write a musical in which Michael Bash was involved. That is how we met. To think that Michael and I would have anything in common, much less extremely compatible religious beliefs, would be as far-fetched as thinking a sci-fi/fantasy author would end up assisting with a book on religion.

You see, our differences are many. Michael has children older than I, so it is not as though we grew up during the same time period. Michael was raised in the Jewish faith, while I was raised in a Christian household. Michael's background is in engineering, while mine is more concentrated in the arts.

Still, after we met, our conversations drifted to a subject about which we are both passionate—religion. I have always been at odds with the majority of my family's belief structure, which leans heavily toward Christian Fundamentalism, and has never sat well with me.

I have never been able to do the "It's-in-the-Bible-so-just-believe-it" thing. In fact, the more I read the Bible, the more the inconsistencies nagged at my brain. I remember one conversation I had with my grandmother. She asked me why I was always questioning the Bible. Why could I not simply follow what God said in His book? My answer to that was simple. I said, "Well, I think that, had God not wanted me to question His book, He would not have given me freedom of thought."

And that is what I found in the mind of Michael Bash—a man willing to break from the conventions of the *standard* religions. To move from what he is told to believe to doing the research for himself. He is a man who is not only willing to ask questions, he is willing to accept the answers he finds.

- Maxwell Alexander Drake - Las Vegas, August 2012

INTRODUCTION

Ehyeh! (Eh-heh-yéh) It's a strange sounding word, yet capable of changing the world.

Ehyeh! Its true meaning was corrupted by a mistranslation more than a millennium ago, and, to this day, remains a well-kept secret. Only recently did I discover the magnitude of its power. My primary goal for publishing this book is to reveal its full significance to the world, at last, and, by doing so, accomplish the following:

1) Settle the contentious debate over evolution, and finally achieve a peaceful accord between science and religion;

2) Restore the importance of God's role in the lives of millions;

3) Set the younger generation of Christians and Jews on an exciting path toward spirituality and harmony; and

4) Present reasonable evidence of God's existence.

Ehyeh! Throughout these pages, you will learn the remarkable history of this word, its vast implications for the universe, and its ultimate impact on our understanding and perception of God, the Bible, and all mankind.

Ehyeh! You will also learn about the Oral Bible as an instrument for updating, where necessary, the written version, yet without diminishing belief in its message. You will discover how, by overlooking this essential tool, Christianity and its principles have remained stuck in the Bronze Age. For religion to be effective and ultimately remain relevant, it must evolve at the same pace as the humanity it serves.

Ehyeh! A personal God who hears and answers our prayers is a difficult concept for many to accept. Certainly, deists do not believe in His existence, nor can many scientists envision Him answering millions of prayers simultaneously. And yet, I have uncovered proof that He can. Within these pages, you will read about Him as a social medium. And that, in fact, God is alive and Googling.

Ehyeh! Additional essays deal with other controversial issues on the topic of the Bible and our general belief systems pertaining to religion and science. It is my conviction that by opening your mind to these new ways of looking at old ideas, you will come away refreshed and renewed in your view of the world and of your particular role in its evolution.

Ehyeh! Why do I repeat this extraordinary word seven times? Any fewer, and you may not have gotten the message.

- Michael Bash - Los Angeles, August 2012

"The most beautiful thing we can experience is the mysterious. It is the source of all true art and science. He to whom the emotion is a stranger, who can no longer pause to wonder and stand wrapped in awe, is as good as dead —his eyes are closed. The insight into the mystery of life, coupled though it be with fear, has also given rise to religion. To know what is impenetrable to us really exists, manifesting itself as the highest wisdom and the most radiant beauty, which our dull faculties can comprehend only in their most primitive forms—this knowledge, this feeling is at the center of true religiousness. In this sense, and in this sense alone, I am a devoutly religious man."

- Albert Einstein

CHAPTER ONE
FINDING COMMON GROUND

How does science and religion complement each other, you ask? Well, that is a very good question.

But before I can answer that—better yet, before you are ready to accept my answer—we should set some ground rules.

If you are a religious fundamentalist, and you truly believe that the Bible is the very Word of God and therefore infallible, you need to open your mind. Any person of intelligence has to admit there are inconsistencies in the Bible. Be assured, by this admission, you are not weakening your faith, nor are you diminishing religion or God.

Remember, if you have faith in God, then you must have faith that He knew what He was doing when He developed the Bible. So, if there are inconsistencies, and you deny their existence, are you not also denying God's purpose by His declarations? By considering yourself an atheist based on lack of proof of a creator God, you can still be sufficiently open-minded to any new potential evidence to come your way.

To this end, I ask believer and non-believer alike to read Exodus 3:14. Many interpretations vary in their interpretation of this transcendental passage.

The New International Version (©1984), New Living Translation (©2007), English Standard Version (©2001), New American Standard Bible (©1995), GOD'S WORD® Translation (©1995), and World English Bible all publish the following translation:

God said to Moses, "I AM WHO I AM."

The King James Bible (Cambridge Ed.), King James 2000

Bible (©2003), American King James Version, American Standard Version, Darby Bible Translation, English Revised Version, and Webster's Bible Translation use this translation:

And God said unto Moses, "I AM THAT I AM."

Douay-Rheims Bible gives the following as the translation:

God said to Moses, "I AM WHO AM."

And the Young's Literal Translation provides the following:

And God saith unto Moses, "I AM THAT WHICH I AM."

The problem is, in the original Hebrew, the term used here—*Ehyeh Asher Ehyeh*—has a vastly different connotation than its commonly accepted translation, *I am*. The Hebrew word for "I am" is *heenenee*. By contrast, Ehyeh Asher Ehyeh, literally translated, means, "I will be what I will be" or "I shall be what I shall be."

The worst thing about this mistranslation is that the word Ehyeh is used 43 times in the Old Testament and only here, in this one passage, is it translated wrong. In all other passages it is defined as, "I will be (or I shall be)." To add fuel to this argument, just two passages earlier, in Exodus 3:12, the word is used properly when God says, *I will be with you*. So, there are two separate passages, in close proximity, both using the same word, but with extremely different significance. And yet this corrupted and clearly inconsistent version of the Bible has survived multiple generations of modernized updates all across the globe.

However, in several translations of the Bible (such as the NIV, IBS, and New Living Translation Bibles), a small footnote has emerged, acknowledging that Ehyeh may also be translated as: *I will (shall) be that which I will (shall) be.*

You might be wondering why the fact of this misinterpretation may be important to our two warring factions, but if you consider the ramifications of this passage's intent, the battle is over.☙

☙ For the creationist fundamentalist: You say the Bible is

the Word of God, and therefore infallible. Well, I submit to you that God, in *His* original words (not the varied translations made thousands of years afterward), more accurately transmitted the message: *I am evolving.*

This one Bible mistranslation of the many represents nothing less than a game-changer for the atheist perspective, which asks, if God is perfect, why does He continue to change throughout the Bible? It also puts to rest the controversy over the age of the earth and the creation of Man. If God is evolving and Man is made in His image, it follows then that Man, too, evolves.

Now, consider what God said to Moses in the following verse: *Say to the Israelites: "The Lord, the God of your fathers — the God of Abraham, the God of Isaac and the God of Jacob — has sent me to you." This is my name forever, the name you shall call me from generation to generation.*

Take a moment to consider the impact of this passage on your belief system. First, God appeared to be saying that He was evolving. Then, in essence, He commanded: *This is what you will call me forever, what your children will call me, what your grandchildren will call me, etc., etc. for all of eternity.* Basically, this would be like me introducing myself as Michael, and from then on, you choosing to call me Bob.

For the atheist fundamentalist: You say there is no God because no one can show you irrefutable proof. Remember, these passages were written at the end of the Bronze Age, when people still had no idea how the sun rose and set each day. Also, remember that people of that day — for that matter, even people of today — had difficulty accepting an imperfect God, which likely accounts for the mistranslation.

Can you not accept the *possibility* that if someone wrote about evolution during the Bronze Age, perhaps they knew something of the concept of human creation that was as yet unfathomable to the rest of the population?

A more contemporary example of this would be a

child asking his parents where he came from. In order to frame an answer to accommodate their child's innocence, parents would generally explain the process on its most basic level.

The same rule as easily holds true for the Bible. When the people asked God how they came to be, He wove His explanation into a simple allegory: *God made man from the dust of the ground.* (Genesis 2:7). Is that not the simplest description of evolution you have ever read? Whereas you have been educated to accept that mankind evolved over millions, if not billions, of years, Bronze Age man, who did not even understand how the moon suspends in space, would certainly have had no way to conceptualize the passage of so much time.

But a question remains. Why would some intelligent entity have offered such a simple explanation unless He also knew that the facts were too complex for the people to understand?

So try to open your mind to the possibility that there was a greater intelligence at work 3,300 years ago than can be accounted for within the general population. Not only did someone from that period write about an evolving God, he also tried—and failed—to pass along God's true name from generation to generation.

Imagine! Someone proposed a scientific concept at a time when science was generally viewed as little more than sorcery, and additionally asked the reader to pass it along forever, knowing that mankind's knowledge and comprehension would not catch up with the facts for several millennia.

While you may not fully accept the line of reasoning I have proposed in this chapter, surely, as a pragmatic thinker, neither can you readily dismiss the argument. ⌀

CHAPTER TWO
THE EVOLVING BIBLE
ORAL LAW

The Bible was given by God to Moses on Mount Sinai, and was read and practiced by the Jews for 1,000 years. It was initially understood among scholars that the Bible was not a complete text, so an Oral Law was developed and updated over a 500-year period, based on the verbal principles originally conveyed on Mount Sinai. These laws clarified the Written Bible with explanations and interpretations of the text.

Eventually, the Oral Bible was transcribed into written  form as the Talmud. Much later, in 1563, the Shulchan Aruch (literally translated from Hebrew as: "Set Table") was written as the Code of Jewish Law. Along with its commentaries, which were updated on an ongoing basis until as recently as 100 years ago, the Shulchan Aruch is considered the most widely accepted compilation of Jewish law ever written.

Ultimately, believers in the "literal truth" of the Bible have been believers in the literal truth of nothing more than a translation. The pure meaning of a word resonates truest with those people who claim it as part of their living language. Modern day vernacular is often mistranslated from one's native idiom into one that is less familiar and, in the process, risks missing the mark completely. A good example is President John F. Kennedy's famous speech on his visit to Berlin, and the oft-quoted statement he made to the people, "Ich bin ein Berliner." What he meant to say, and what he thought he was saying, was "I am one of you." To a native of Berlin, naturally an expert in contemporary German slang, Kennedy was, more precisely, saying, "I am a hamburger." Whereas it is accurate among Americans to say, "I am a New Yorker" or "I am a Bostonian," the same literal translation does not work in German for "Berliner," as Germans use that particular word to refer to the popular ground beef sandwich. In that same vein, even an American would know better than to speak to a group from Frankfurt and say, "I am a Frankfurter."

Two thousand years ago, when Christianity adopted the Bible, they were apparently unaware of the Oral Law, and therefore had no way of taking advantage of its wisdom and logic. Had they done so at the time, they would have realized that the Bible was not to be taken literally—and for a valid reason.

Life evolves. People evolve. And, as they do, so does their understanding. Every generation is more knowledgeable than the previous. So, it is inconceivable to expect that any book dealing with the world around us and written for the people of one generation to equally apply to succeeding generations in perpetuity. For example, a book written 100 years ago on the subject of courting practices between men and women would sound blatantly archaic, even laughable, to people of today with our 21st century sensibilities.

As life evolves, so, too, must the Bible. Because the Oral Bible provides the Written Bible with permission to evolve, adapt, and upgrade to accommodate subsequent generations, there is no reason to adhere to the literal truth when simple logic plainly advises against it.

"Every one who is seriously involved in the pursuit of science becomes convinced that a spirit is manifest in the laws of the Universe-a spirit vastly superior to that of man, and one in the face of which we with our modest powers must feel humble. In this way the pursuit of science leads to a religious feeling of a special sort, which is indeed quite different from the religiosity of someone more naïve."

- Albert Einstein

CHAPTER THREE
IS THERE A WAR

Between Science and Religion?
Science versus Spirituality?

In their new book, *War of the Worldviews*, Deepak Chopra and Leonard Mlodinow discuss the controversial topic of science versus spirituality, each from his own perspective as spiritualist and scientist, respectively. More predictably, they might have titled their book, *War Between Science and Religion*, but the fact that they took religion out of the equation is what sets their thought-provoking book apart from the rest of the herd.

On the subject of evolution, Chopra says: "Evolution is the club that science wielded to beat religion into the dust, and whenever religious ideas threaten to take on new life, science rushes in to smash them down again. These ideas include, first and foremost, the perfection of God. According to religion, the deity didn't need to get smarter, because God is omniscient...Having declared the creator perfect,

I will be that which I will be

religion couldn't call God's creation imperfect: therefore, the universe didn't need to evolve, either." And that is the basis for the church's centuries-long ignorance of the facts.

The irony of Chopra's statement, that the belief in God's perfection precludes his need to evolve, while based on the commonly held perception of God, is diametrically opposite to how God identified Himself to Moses when they met on Mount Sinai in Exodus 3:14 and He told him, *"I will be that which I will be...This is my name forever."* That declaration by God meant the same then as it has always meant, that He claimed not to be perfect, but, rather, to be evolving. When the Greeks were adapting the Bible to their own language, the translators would not accept the concept that God was not already perfect so they chose to mistranslate His all-important message to read: *I am that I am,* erroneously signifying that He was already a full and complete deity—i.e., *perfect.* An extreme distortion of God's meaning, and yet, "I am that I am" has remained the option of the faithful ever since, despite clear evidence to the contrary. The fact that all subsequent Bible translations have been made from the Greek, and not the original Hebrew, explains, in large part, the perpetuation of this transformative error.

In more recent English translations, recognition is often given the accurate Hebrew translation, but only in tiny footnotes. What would happen if everyone who read these words did his homework and discovered for himself the magnitude of this 3,300-year old mistake? First and foremost, the brutal and lengthy battle between science and religion/spirituality would come to a screeching halt, and all literary material on the subject, voluminous as it is, would become instantly obsolete. Ultimately, of course, peace would reign between the two diverse schools of thought, and progress would follow as they agreed to pool their collective knowledge for the ultimate advancement of society. ֍

Yet, one particular problem with religion might remain, as it is based on dogma that is fixed in time, and therefore closed to change or modification, even in the face of new understanding. By contrast, at the basis of science is the quest for discovery that increases our knowledge of the universe and the species that inhabit its space. It would seem by definition that the two were mutually exclusive. And yet, unlike the static chapter and verse of the written Bible, the Oral Bible is structured to accept, modify, and update its text to accommodate new findings and greater understanding. Through the Oral Bible, the Jewish people are constantly questioning aspects of the Mosaic Laws and adapting fresh thoughts and ideas, including scientific discovery, to accommodate the increasing awareness of their respective generation.

By the time Christianity was established, the Oral Bible (or the Talmud), had already existed for 1,500 years. But it was not incorporated into the new religion's holy texts—most probably because it did not exist in written form until 500 years after the Christian Bible was developed. Had early Christians been able to read and accept the Oral Bible, the concept of "literal truth" would never have had a place in their religious dogma. Nor would there exist, even now, the fundamental belief in a 6,000-year-old universe, as interpreted from the Book of Genesis, yet completely disproven by modern scientific discovery.

Despite the insightful and provocative arguments posed by Chopra and Mlodinow in their *War of the Worldviews*, I hold little expectation that those billions of believers across the planet would choose to substitute a spiritual existence for the ongoing comfort and security they receive from their unyielding belief in a loving and all-powerful "perfect" God.

CHAPTER FOUR
COMMON
MISCONCEPTIONS

About the Bible

In an article published in the CNN Belief Blog, John Spong, a former Episcopal bishop of Newark, New Jersey writes about three major misconceptions that he believes diminish the Bible's credibility.

The first misconception on the part of the faithful relates to their assumption that the Bible accurately reflects history: Spong is correct in his assessment here. A large segment of the world population regards the Bible as a history

book rather than what it is, which is a storybook based loosely on events that are said to have taken place in the ancient world over the course of a few thousand years. Whichever way the Bible is viewed, as fiction or factual, it does not diminish its inexorable power to inspire, teach, and perpetuate an extraordinary sense of pride in the fathers of the people of Israel.

A second misconception, according to Bishop Spong, is the contention that the Bible is, in any literal sense, the Word of God. This theory seems to have arisen from the Bible's depiction of God as punishing the Egyptians by sending them the Ten Plagues. He also helped Joshua (Joshua 10:12) kill more Amorites by temporarily stopping the movement of the sun. And He ordered King Saul (1 Samuel 15:1-35) to commit genocide against the Amalekites. Further evidence to support Spong's theory is found in the death penalties issued for disobedience of God's laws—major and minor alike. "What kind of God would that be?" the bishop asks.

I contend that Bishop Spong is wrong, however, in his overall analysis. He is making the same mistake as other contemporary writers have made repeatedly, including Richard Dawkins, Victor Stenger, and the late Christopher Hitchens. They have all based their successful careers on criticizing the 3,300-year old text—which was written specifically for the primitive people of the Bronze Age—while making their case through the lens of their modern sensibilities. Let's consider a very important concept. Anyone writing a book dedicated to influencing a large number of people, in order to make it successful, must know what his readership wants to read and then set about to meet those needs. The end result would be a book that conveys stories and/or principles intended to garner admiration, credibility, respect, and, ultimately, acceptance. In terms of the Bible, if it had instead provoked controversy and anger, it would long ago have been burned to ashes and its writer(s) condemned. Clearly, that has not been the case, as the Bible is still the world's most beloved text. Not only has it survived, it has flourished, and is more popular than ever after 3,300 years.

You can't argue with success. The Bible is the most successful book ever written, with 25 billion copies sold to date, and is the indisputable spiritual foundation for our three major religions, consisting of four billion believers all across the globe. What accounts for the Bible's phenomenal achievement? One has to consider it was written effectively for the people of the time. They admired and respected a

17

God who dealt ruthlessly with idol worshippers and with those who disobeyed His laws, regardless of how minor. While it is difficult for us to understand the acceptance of wholesale brutality within its chapters, the results speak for themselves, and they are hard to argue. If the Bible had depicted God in the beginning as loving and merciful, it would have diminished His more crucial image as an all-powerful and all-knowing deity. Might was right, after all. And isn't it still?

I would argue with Bishop Spong's conclusion that God could not have written the Bible. While we have no proof in either direction, whoever did the writing, and it was likely more than one author, possessed incredible insights into the psychology of the people and was therefore able to convey precisely what they wanted to hear while engaging their emotions and capturing their eternal faith. That was indeed an enormous accomplishment, one that few prize-winning authors today would feel qualified to challenge.

Let's assume that tomorrow someone wrote a book about a God-fearing man named Abraham who instructed his oldest and most trusted assistant to go out into the world and find his son Isaac an exemplary wife, and to solemnly swear himself to the task, not by putting his hand on a Bible, as is now standard procedure, but "under his thigh." (Genesis 24:2) We would recoil at the notion of a man of such august stature exhibiting such tasteless, even shocking, behavior. Our modern sensibilities would dictate we dismiss the revelation as mere fiction. The concept seems as outrageous to us as if the president of the United States were to swear in a Chief Justice by commanding him to place his hand under his thigh while the entire process was electronically streamed

18

live across the civilized world. So, while many biblical stories resemble fantasy to us, the Bible was accepted as absolutely factual 2,000 years ago. And for those 2.5 billion Christians living today, every single story contained in both Old and New Testaments, regardless of how remotely they compare with our secular belief systems, still hold up as 100% fact, and, indeed, the Word of God.

All this goes to prove that in order to spread faith you need only to convince one or two generations of your message. Thereafter, each succeeding generation brainwashes the next. Ad infinitum. Once set in stone, there is no amount of logic or contradictory evidence in this universe to reason believers out of a belief they acquired in childhood. Regardless of their intelligence and the apparent absurdity of their convictions (i.e., a 6,000-year-old universe) they will steadfastly hold to their argument. Such is the power of faith and the spiritual comfort it provides.

A third and major misconception cited by Spong is that biblical truth is static and unchanging. This particular notion came about because the Christians received the Bible from the Jews, who had already followed it for over 1,000 years. But in adopting it for their church's use, the early Christians failed to incorporate the Oral Bible into their teachings because it had not yet been reduced to written form, and was later too much in conflict with the church tenets already locked in place. For the Jews, however, the oral form had long been a necessary part of religious dogma, as it was and is the instrument through which the Written Bible is updated, as time passes and worldviews experience change.

One of the changes made by the Oral Bible was permission to charge interest on a business loan, which was forbidden in the original version of the Bible. This archaic law is still practiced by Muslims, and has been the basis for many problems inherent in their banking system. Various complicated methods were devised over the years to bypass the untenable law, which ultimately inhibits the ability to successfully conduct business. According to www.Wikipedia.com, Sharia Law "prohibits the fixed or floating payment or acceptance of specific interest or fees (known as Riba or usury) for loans of money. Investing in businesses that provide goods or services considered contrary to Islamic principles is also Haraam (forbidden). While these principles may have been applied to historical Islamic economies, it is only in the late 20th century that a number of Islamic banks were formed to apply these principles to private or semi-private commercial institutions within the Muslim community."

I would have to dispute Bishop Spong's opinion that the Bible is not about religion. The first four of the Ten Commandments, as presented to Moses, very clearly express God's requirements of His people. In demanding their reverence, the commandments dictate: 1) there be no other gods before Him, 2) no worshipping of false idols, 3) the Sabbath day must be kept holy, and 4) the Lord's name must not be taken in vain. These laws are religious in nature, and show no trace of secular sensibilities.

Bishop Spong's article goes on to postulate that the Bible evolves, based on the fact that God is depicted differently over the course of some 1,000 years—from angry and vengeful to righteous and benevolent. By the time Christianity was founded, God had become a universal God, all-loving and forgiving. But this variation in God's image can be attributed significantly to the understanding that the Bible was probably written by several authors over a protracted period, during which time man had become somewhat more worldly and knowledgeable, as reflected in their depiction of the Deity. Even in the second book of the Old Testament (Exodus 3:14) God made his promise to forever evolve into the future. And as the good former Bishop Spong explains, God has kept his promise. ❡

CHAPTER FIVE
REALIZATION AND ALTERATION

Resolving the Battle Between
Science and Religion

When I graduated from NJIT (New Jersey Institute of Technology) with a BS degree in Electrical Engineering, I immediately went to work for Weston Electrical Instrument Company in Newark, New Jersey. I learned all about electrical instruments very quickly and soon began developing a series of inventions for which I obtained patents. One in particular became world-famous and brought in millions of dollars for Weston Electric. (Patent Pending 1960; Final Patent 1965.)

One of these inventions was a fail-safe device that would activate an alarm whenever it detected trouble within the instrument. It took me a long time and many experiments to develop the elaborate circuitry system that triggered its functionality. When my work was completed, company executives attended a special demonstration and showered me with praise for my ingenuity. I was even given a raise. Several months later, a competing company filed for bankruptcy and promptly went out of business. Weston Electric hired two of their best engineers. When I demonstrated my fail-safe device to one of them, he told me my design was far too complicated, and that his company had developed a much simpler one that accomplished the same thing. When he showed me the better design, which, in retrospect, seemed so obvious, I felt embarrassed and stupid for not having thought of it on my own. I cite this story because whenever I observe religious people and scientists stating and restating their stale respective arguments before the court of public opinion, I am invariably reminded of my fail-safe invention.

There are a few ways through which people can understand the intersection of science and religion. One is conflict in which advocates of either side publish endless numbers of articles, books, and essays that lay out their case—much like a contest in which there can emerge only one winner. It would seem to come down to one ultimately making his case better than the other and unilaterally declaring victory.

Another view is that science and religion can never be in conflict because they are distinct and independent of each other—belonging to different magisteria. *Science asks how and religion asks why.* It's rather like comparing apples and oranges.

The third option is a dialogue in which science and religion try to learn from each other.

The fourth and final view is what I call "Realization and Alteration," requiring science and religion to come together devoid of conflict and become an integral blend of a person's worldview. This is the enlightened perspective I hope we can all achieve sooner or later. Realization and

Alteration is really the one way—and, I believe, the right way—to end this contentious tug-of-war that neither side can ever win unconditionally. ❧

Before the birth of science the accepted view of the universe and the origin of man was set forth in the Bible, which dealt with moral laws as well as the creation of the universe and mankind. There was no controversy at the time because all such information came from one source—the Bible. And, because the church had so strong an influence over the people, the Bible was considered the ultimate source of knowledge, and therefore indisputable.

The problem began when science was born, and broadcasted its findings to the people. Suddenly, a conflict arose because science was expressing ideas that were diametrically opposed to those in the Bible. Why the discrepancy? Because science had grown out of an evolving body of experience and knowledge, whereas the Book of Genesis was terminally stuck in the ancient past and shut off from changing times and perspectives. If all existing knowledge of modern science had been established at the same time the Bible was being written, it would have been integrated into its text, and would not have been stirring conflict these many years. Whoever wrote the Bible—God or man—wanted people to believe, cherish, and respect it, and be influenced by its laws and values. So, it was written for that purpose. It spoke to the people of 3,300 years ago with stories about the creation of the world and humankind that connected with their limited knowledge, and instilled in them a sense of pride. It also depicted God in a way that He would be revered and admired.

Sensibilities may change drastically, even in as short a period as 100 years. I recently read a book published early in the 20th century that dispensed advice on etiquette. From my 21st century perspective, I found it hilarious. If it had been written 3,300 years ago, it would have seemed even more outlandish. How can a young science argue with an ancient text? It would be tantamount to teaching college calculus to a pre-school toddler and expecting him to get a passing grade.

One of the biggest obstacles to peace between science and religion is the Genesis story of Creation. It is important to remember that Genesis was written for a generation that lacked the capacity to conceive of a 13.7 billion-years-old universe. In arguing for the credibility of the Bible, some scholars have claimed to read hints of codes in the narrative that reflect the true age of the universe. But none of this is necessary. The Bible does not need to be defended.

How can any intelligent, educated person rationally contend that the Genesis stories are based on fact? Does anyone think that God, or whoever wrote the Bible, would have been able to explain that the universe was billions of years old and then proceed to describe the principles of evolution as we understand them today? And if the author had written it this way, would the Bible have become the successful book it has remained?

As with my fail-safe device, there is a much simpler solution to the conflict between science and religion than we have heard thus far. An endless number of books and articles have been written by scholars and distinguished members of clergy to defend their own position and attack the opposition. They advance their argument using complicated methodology like intelligent design. Motivated politically to introduce books into the nation's school systems that defend their inflexible biblical position, they have spent millions of dollars over the years to influence government leaders to their cause. All to no avail. And the war rages on.

ᶿ To illustrate how Realization and Alteration plays out in everyday life, I offer the following story: My CPA and I are personal friends, and we meet for lunch two or three times a week. Several years ago, he lost a lot of weight. Because he takes pride in his appearance, he bought an expensive suit to accommodate his slimmer figure. When he wore it to lunch one day, he looked very distinguished and naturally received a bevy of compliments. Then, over the ensuing years, he regained the twenty pounds he had lost and is now back to his normal weight.

Recently, he wore that same magnificent suit to lunch, and he looked terrible. The suit no longer fit him, and the buttons on his jacket looked like they were ready to pop. I recommended that he take the suit to his tailor for alterations. At first he argued that the suit still looked good on him—that all he had to do was leave the jacket unbuttoned. But by the time lunch was over, he agreed with me. The next time I saw him for lunch he was wearing the elegant suit, newly altered. It now fit him to perfection—even better than it had originally, when he was too slim. And the compliments have resumed.

The Holy Bible, like a suit of clothes, was designed to be altered to fit man as he evolves. When the Book of Genesis was written, the Bible was the perfect fit for man's narrow range of knowledge. Over the course of the next 3,300 years, however, man gained substantially in an understanding of his place in the universe, and has since outgrown the original Bible. People of faith today must realize that the way to make the Bible fit for a more universally knowledgeable readership is to alter it accordingly from time to time.

When a scientist makes a statement about the universe, it is based on evidence. When a religious person makes a statement about the universe and quotes the Bible for evidence, he is basing the argument on his interpretation of God's truth. But when that same religious individual acknowledges

that God had no choice but to express Himself as he did in the Bible in order to engage the intellect and sensibilities of the ancient people for whom He wrote, the controversy immediately evaporates, and an alteration to the law becomes the realistic solution.

The U.S. Constitution offers a strong comparison to the Bible. At the time it was written, it set forth certain laws relative to our newly founded nation. But almost immediately thereafter, in 1791, our lawmakers began to realize there were vital issues not previously addressed in the Constitution, so they passed a series of ten amendments that became known as the Bill of Rights, and which were written to protect our citizens' natural rights of liberty and property. Without these amendments and those to follow over the ensuing centuries, we would be living under an entirely different set of rules.

The U.S. Constitution and the Bible: one is a living document, adjustable to the times in which we live, and one remains stubbornly rooted in the obsolete and limited sensibilities of an ancient world. In order to resolve this long-standing conflict that remains locked into a stalemate, the following steps must be taken: ∅

REALIZATION

∅ 1) **Realize that the Bible was written at a level to be accepted and admired by the ancient people of 3,300 years ago.**

2) **Realize that the Bible came with a companion guide, The Oral Bible — an essential instrument with the primary function to continually update specific entries in the Bible in order to maintain relevancy for an ever-evolving human race.**

26

3) Realize that God told Moses that He evolves: "I will be that which I will be." (Exodus 3:14) If God evolves, which He says He does, and we are made in His image, which He says we are, there is no other conclusion to reach other than that we, also, evolve.

4) Realize the fact that God describes Himself as evolving is also strong indication that He exists. What human author 3,300 years ago would have described God in this way? The sensibilities to make such an observation had not yet been developed. Even today it is extremely hard for people to see God as evolving.

ALTERATION

The only two simple revisions the Bible currently needs are:

1) A small modification to Genesis 1:1: *In the beginning, many billions of years ago, God created the heavens and earth.* This new time frame eliminates the foolish concept of a 6,000-year-old universe.

2) A footnote to the story of the creation of Adam and Eve: *This story was created for the understanding of an ancient people. The facts reveal that man was actually created from earth by means of an evolutionary process that took several billion years and continues to this day.*

By referencing evolution in the Adam and Eve story, the conflict between science and religion would necessarily come to a screeching halt. An additional footnote to the allegorical story of Adam and Eve bears mentioning here. The Tree of Knowledge and its impact on Adam and Eve symbolizes humanity's evolutionary journey. God evolved the single cell into

a multiple-cell organism, which slowly evolved into an intelligent species of creatures with full awareness of themselves and their place in the universe—an exclusively human quality. One could argue that God did not approve of the human species possessing this level of knowledge because it also meant we would be required to experience suffering. Assuming, then, that Adam and Eve represent the allegory of evolution, it is also possible to perceive their mortal sin, not as the result of a single act of transgression, but as a collective or accumulated sin that is ongoing.

The Bible contradicts itself repeatedly in describing what have come to be known as the first man and woman on earth. In Genesis 5:1, it states, to the effect: *When God created man He made him in His likeness. He created them male and female and blessed them, and...He called them "Adam."* In the preceding Genesis 4:13, it states: *Cain said to the Lord... "I will be a restless wanderer on the earth, and whoever finds me will kill me."* In response to Cain's expression of fear, Genesis 4:15 reads: *The Lord said to him, "Not so. If anyone kills Cain, he will suffer vengeance seven times over." Then the Lord put a mark on Cain so that no one who found him would kill him.* But besides his parents, who else was there on earth to "find and kill" him? The Bible never explains this glaring discrepancy.

If the story of Genesis is ever to be accepted as allegorical in nature, it should follow that other Bible stories should be equally reframed. John Polkinghorne, in his book, *Science and Religion in Quest of Truth*, described biblical allegory or symbolism as "a way of expressing truth too deep to be expressed in any other form than story." As an example of this genre, he cited the Fall in Genesis 3. "Read literally as an account of a simple, disastrous ancestral event that brought death into the world, it is clearly incompatible with what we now know about the evolution of hominids.

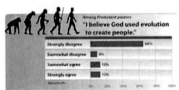 Read symbolically, it conveys profound insight."

I wonder why no one ever asked why God did not want man to know about Good and Evil. My guess is that He did not want us to experience suffering, although it would seem virtually impossible to avoid on this earth as we know it to have been created. We tend to assume that God is omnipotent, but that cannot be true. He is seriously restricted by the limitations built into the system. The issue of suffering is particularly troublesome to people of faith, who invariably ask, *"Why did God let that happen?"* We can only assume that God knows human suffering is part of the process of living, and is powerless to alter His own system.

It boggles the mind that so many millions of people decry evolution. Evidence of its existence is all around us. Think about it. Is God capable of instantly creating a living human out of a fertilized egg? No. The process of creating a viable human being takes nine months from conception to delivery. With the exception of Adam, of whom it is written He created in one day, the nine-month cycle was true even in the case of God's own son, Jesus. The process required God to inseminate a woman—Mary—who would carry the embryo through its normal phases of development over the requisite number of months. It would seem that human suffering is governed, and therefore limited, by the same set of laws.

The biggest conflict between religion and science is evolution, for the following three reasons: 1) it is demeaning to man to accept the concept that we evolved from a lower species of animal, 2) the Bible says that God created man from earth, and 3) evolution is generally referenced as a theory rather than a fact, which provides for the possibility that it is no more than an idea. Other theories, like that of relativity, are more generally accepted because they do not involve our egos or question our religious faith. It is interesting to note that ultimately it is God who makes the case for evolution in Exodus 3:14.

If God evolves, then mankind, created in His image, evolves, too. It's a simple case of cause and effect. This fundamental view is so entrenched in religious doctrine that it leaves the question of evolution irrelevant. So, despite God's assertion that this is His name forever, and that it is to be passed down from generation to generation, the mistranslation is accepted as accurate, and evolution as false.

ACTIVATION

Once religion adopts a worldview that accepts and embraces evolution as an integral part of the Bible, the root cause for conflict ceases to exist, and harmony becomes the prevailing wisdom. ◊

CHAPTER SIX
WHERE ON EARTH IS GOD?

Therefore my people will know my name; therefore in that day they will know that it is I who foretold it. Yes, IT IS I. (Isaiah 52:6)

Today's literary marketplace is inundated with the thinking of popular atheists, including Richard Dawkins, Victor Stenger, the late Christopher Hitchens, and illustrious others — all singing their traditional theme song, *"Show me the evidence and I'll believe."* In a world that is increasingly influenced by science, their skepticism makes sense, since we have no concrete evidence that God actually exists. God is God, after all, and if He really has the capacity to appear before us in an instant — to believers and nonbelievers alike — why hasn't He done so and finally put to rest this ongoing controversy that questions His existence? We all know it's been 2,000 years since we've heard anything from Him, and yet when Moses, the prophets, and Jesus were around, He was at their constant beck and call. Is it something we said? And if so, what?

Over a period of months while writing a number of essays regarding God and the Bible, the question of God's absence plagued me constantly. I could not come up with a plausible reason to justify His remaining so out of touch over the millennia. I even referred to

Exodus 3:14, in which God revealed His name to Moses in Hebrew as Ehyeh Asher Ehyeh, which He shortened to Ehyer. Despite the background noise of the burning bush, He managed to emphasize to Moses the importance of His name being remembered forever. Understanding human nature as well as He did, He knew it would take a while for His name to catch on. But, as we already know, in spite of God's explicit instructions, it got lost in translation.

One has to conclude that this inconsistency was more than an error in proofreading. The concept of an evolving God was, first of all, an inconceivable concept to the Bronze Age population, and secondly, it came with the potential for game-changing consequences. Why? Because if God evolves, that means He is not yet perfect. What kind of implication does that have on the Judeo-Christian tradition seeking an almighty deity? Only enormous.

Last night I had a dream in which my late wife came to me and said: "I see you are writing a book about God. Publish it as soon as you can. You will convince all believers of the Bible to begin calling God by His real name. I see young people wearing "Ehyeh" T-shirts in many shapes and colors. I see His name on billboards, buses, cars, planes, and trains. I hear poems praising Ehyeh with powerful slogans, "Hallelujah, Ehyeh, forever and ever," and popular songs in His name flooding the media." Ehyeh could even have His own Facebook page, Twitter account, and YouTube video.

Was that just a crazy dream I had or was it something else? I wonder.

That was not the first time I heard from my late wife in the form of a dream, and each time she has visited me so far her messages turned out to be accurate. So, maybe we can all get together and make this dream of mine come true for the sake of mankind. Maybe if we follow God's commandment to remember His name, He would respond and unequivocally make known His presence. While the faithful need no such evidence, the rest of us would do well with a little black-and-white clarity. In either case, a visit from God would dispel the disharmony between both schools of thought, and ultimately generate a collective call for rejoicing.

Let's do it the 21st century way. Let's use the power of the Internet and person-to-person marketing to convey our vital message. Let's teach His real name to billions of people and fulfill the prophesy in Isaiah 11:9: *For the earth will be full of the knowledge of God as the waters cover the sea.*

As incredible as it sounds, I firmly believe that if we were all to call God by His real name with full understanding of its significance, somehow, from somewhere, we would hear from Him in a manner provable by science. In that moment, we would know with certainty that God exists and, at the same time, He would know that the human race has finally caught onto the significance of His name and the absolute truth of His essence. This could be an exciting project: infusing energy, enthusiasm, and hope into the great multitudes of young people and old all across the face of the globe. Imagine America as "One nation under Ehyeh." Or singing "Ehyeh Bless America" while their British counterparts intone "Ehyeh Save the Queen."

The future is definitely looking up. ◆

CHAPTER SEVEN
COMMON SENSE

The Seeds of Evolution Are
Rooted in Genesis

A war rages across our planet Earth. A war that has endured for centuries—since well before the time that the Catholic Church arrested Galileo for heresy in the early 1600s. This is essentially a bloodless war between science and religion in which the combatants range from every level of involvement, although the loudest participants are the extremists of each opposing group.

On the religious side, the creationist fundamentalists raise their bullhorns and scream: "God is perfect, so the Bible is perfect. I reject your logic of science!"

On the scientific side are the atheist fundamentalists with clipboards and microscopes, saying: "Show me the proof. If I can't touch it, it must be false!" The main conflict of this war is, "Does God really exist?" The weapon of choice for both sides is the Bible—the Old and New Testaments.

Those who fight on the side of religion believe they are defending the Bible—the holy book, composed by God himself—every sentence of which is a heavenly creation, to be understood literally as the absolute truth. For God does not make mistakes.

Those who fight on the side of science claim to be defending logic. They contend it is absurd for anyone to believe in something that can't be experienced with any of the five senses, and yet they reject the facts that are right in front of their noses. By attempting to discredit the Bible— they deny the divinity of the Old and New Testaments. Their very goal is to prove, through science, that God is a delusion—that He cannot exist in our modern world.

Both groups fail to take into account the facts that surround the very tool they use to uphold their argument—the Bible. For it is the Bible itself, or more specifically, the way we think about the Bible, that is the root cause for the ongoing conflict.

Let us start there, with the facts surrounding the Bible. Not the words contained within its pages, but with the book's creation itself.

The first fact is that the Bible was developed over a long period of time. Many believe it was written sometime between 1,500 B.C. and 500 B.C., a span of 1,000 years.

Obviously, that would mean that many people, over multiple generations, had a hand in its creation. Keep this fact in mind as we move along.

The second fact is that whoever wrote the Bible—whether it was God, His followers, or simply a group of people with their own agenda—did so with one goal in mind: to influence anyone who read it. It was essential that their readers accept its contents as pure and unadulterated gospel.

Which brings us to fact number three. For the Bible to be convincing, and subsequently successful, it had to be written for—and resonate strongly with—the people of that time. And its appeal had to be greater than for any book previously written, because of the author(s) intention that it live on through the generations.

As it turned out, the manner in which the Old Testament depicted God, His laws, and His commandments, was extremely acceptable to the people of that time. The Bible was venerated, every word cherished, by those who read and believed in it. It was so influential, in fact, that parents fervently taught it to their children so that subsequent generations would continue to revere the Bible as a holy book, and to worship God with all their hearts and souls—just as the author(s) envisioned.

All these facts must be taken into account when discussing the subject.

Now, let's look at a few examples of how these facts are used in heated discourse. ☙

THE INCONSISTENCIES OF GOD

☙ When reading the Bible, you see that God changes as the book progresses. In Genesis, God is a tribal, jealous, vindictive god. As we read on into Jeremiah and Isaiah, we find Him described as a more universal, compassionate god. In the New Testament, He is a loving, self-sacrificing god.

Atheistic fundamentalism argues that this is an inconsistency, and therefore proves God is not real. Creation fundamentalism argues that there is no inconsistency, because the Word of God is infallible. Yet neither takes into account our three facts listed above, leaving both arguments invalid.

The creationists' belief that there is no inconsistency is a difficult argument to maintain, since inconsistency runs throughout. Simply stating, "The Bible has no inconsistencies." does not make it so.

In that case, the atheists win, right? Wrong. The atheist argument does not take into account the three facts referring to how and why the Bible was written. If they were to do so using common sense, they would better understand why the Bible depicts God as it does.

When the Bible was first given to the people, the world was a different place than it was as late as 500 B.C., and certainly today. For one thing, in that earlier period, the human race was more tribal. Clan feuds were more common. For the people of that day to believe in a god, He had to be seen as powerful and decisive. The people needed a deity in whom they could put their faith and trust. Since we already know that the Bible had to be written in a style acceptable to the people of the time, that is exactly how the Book of Genesis depicts God, revealing Him as an authority figure that demanded to be taken seriously.

Yet, as time passed and the human race became stronger and self-sufficient, they needed their deity to be more lawful, more civilized. Which is exactly the way God is depicted in the books of the Bible that were published in later years. Does that mean that this is a different God from the Book of Genesis? Or is it the same God, just adapting Himself to the times?

Moving further along over the years, we find humankind in need of compassion and love—aspiring to a brighter future for the generations to follow. So, as we read the New Testament, we discover a deity who fits into that altruistic mold. Again, is this change proof that the God of the Old Testament is different from the God of the New Testament? I suggest that it simply reveals an ever-evolving God who constantly adjusts to the changing needs of the civilization He serves.

So, does this argument mean the creationists win? Absolutely not! They contend that the Bible has no inconsistencies, and they vehemently defend that notion, ignoring not only the logic of science, but also the very words they are defending. If you are driving through town in a car, you will never convince your fellow passenger he is flying through space in a UFO. It is the same with the Bible. There *is* an inconsistency in how God relates to mankind. Arguing that there is *no* inconsistency is just irrational. And, it is this very illogical thinking that turns away so many people from religion.

Why do the creationists argue this way? My theory is that they do it out of fear—that if they accept the possibility of even one small detail in the Bible being inconsistent, their entire faith-based system crumbles to dust.

However, if you are a person of faith, you can readily use common sense to see that Bible inconsistencies are intentional. If the text had not been written as it was, God would probably not have been so successful in engaging His believers over the centuries.

Therefore, inconsistency does not destroy faith. It simply demonstrates how God works in order to reach out and connect with an ever-evolving society.

If anything, these inconsistencies bolster both sides of the dispute. The creationists can be reassured that they worship a God smart enough to change with the needs of His people. The atheists have cause to be impressed that one book written by many people over a protracted period of time is able to grow and change and thereby remain relevant so many centuries later. Furthermore, it should allow them to, at least, entertain the idea that a higher power may have helped keep the project on course. After all, is it not a cardinal rule of science to keep a hypothesis alive as long as there is even the slightest possibility that it might be proven true?

Which brings us to our next common argument between science and religion. ✐

HOW CAN MODERN MAN BELIEVE WHAT THE BIBLE SAYS?

✐ Another grand argument between the scientific and religious cultures relates to the verbiage used within the Bible. Atheist fundamentalists agree that because the terminology is outdated, this is proof there is no God. By contrast, creationist fundamentalists continue to argue, "The Word of God is infallible!"

If we look at the case from the creationist side, we are once again struck by the fact that any rational human who lives in contemporary society is going to have an issue with some of the biblical text. To simply state, "God is infallible!" does not put an automatic check in the win column for the creationist. It just shows his inability to think for himself.

Let's take the example of the now archaic manner in which a binding promise was made 3,300 years ago when one man provided a loan of money to another. I cannot speak for you, but I would object vehemently to taking an oath by placing my hand under another man's thigh. Nor would I expect him to react favorably. In fact, not only would he not likely give me the loan, he would probably have me arrested for sexual harrassment.

So, does this mean the atheists win? No. Because their argument falls apart without looking at the facts, just as does that of the creationists.

Let us pretend that the Bible was never written, and only just recently did someone get the idea of a personal God. And this person decided to write a book he called the Bible. Yet, for some reason, he chose to write it exactly as the Bible was written 3,300 years ago—same words, same structure, exactly. Would the people of today find such a book credible? Not likely. Rather, it would either be viewed as fantasy fiction, or, if the author insisted it was factual and as passed on to him by his "God," he would quickly be diagnosed as severely delusional. That's because our way of thinking today is naturally more advanced than that of the Bronze Age.

Does this mean that we can't study and learn from the Bible? Not at all. Provided we use common sense, we can read the Bible and understand the intended message without being stuck in the implausible verbiage.

The same logic can be used in reverse. Had Richard Dawkins, a great proponent of atheist fundamentalism, written his book *The God Delusion* 3,300 years ago, he would have been completely misunderstood. Not only would he not have convinced the Bronze Age populous that planet Earth exists within a complex solar system, like billions of other solar systems across the universe, he would probably have been stoned to death as a heretic. It amazes me that an intelligent man like Dawkins, who has written several superior books, is completely blind to the facts surrounding the Bible's creation, and refuses to use basic common sense when making his case.

Which leads me to my number one reason both arguments fail. Not only does neither side take into account the facts surrounding the Bible's creation, both cite very specific sections of the Bible, rather than the whole, with which to validate their arguments.

Atheists criticize the Bible's antiquated ideas and prejudices of 3,300 years ago. Yet, even with their intelligence, they let their emotions overcome their common sense. For the atheists, this is a literary blind spot. The Bible is filled with great wisdom, poetry, and moral values that have little bearing on the argument for or against God's existence. If it were not such a literary triumph on a secular level, as well as spiritual, it would have long ago ceased to be revered by its billions of followers.

The same holds true for creationist fundamentalists and their fear of accepting inconsistency. Controlled by their zeal and their blind faith, they defend the Bible as though it were written for modern man.

We have scientific proof that the universe is approximately 13.7 billion years old. We can formulate a theory about it, then test that theory, and achieve the predicted result. We know that, through evolution, all life on earth was created. Again, this is testable and provable. And, that is how science works. You create a hypothesis, test it, and if you can get the expected answer repeatedly, you trust that the hypothesis is sound.

Were both sides of this controversy to use common sense, they would not feel compelled to defend the Bible or to attack it—they would simply better understand it for what it is.⌂

⌂ Albert Einstein, the greatest scientist of all time, wrote: "The Jewish tradition contains something which finds splendid expression in many of the Psalms—namely, a sort of intoxicated joy and amazement at the beauty and grandeur of this world, of which man can just form a faint notion. It is the feeling from which true scientific research draws its spiritual sustenance." He also wrote: "To me, the Torah (the Five Books of Moses), as interpreted by the Talmud (the Oral Law) is merely the most important evidence for the manner in which the Jewish conception of life held sway in earlier times. The essence of that conception seems to me to lie in an affirmative attitude to the life of all creation. The life of the individual has meaning only in so far as it aids in making the life of every living thing nobler and more beautiful... It is clear also that 'serving God' was equated with 'serving the living.' The best of the Jewish people, especially the Prophets and Jesus, contended tirelessly for this."

The creationists and other religious fundamentalists are well advised to understand that when the Bible (the Torah part) was given to Moses, who then presented it to the elders of Israel, the people had many questions, which Moses set about to answer. Through this question-and-answer process, the Oral Law was created. Religious fundamentalists have yet to understand that the Bible is not complete without the Talmud—it is merely half of the whole—the largely outdated half.

What I am attempting to show in this book is that science and religion complement each other, and benefit mankind by working as a harmonious unit rather than as opposing forces. Anyone with common sense can pursue science and still believe in the existence of God and the divinity of the Bible. Discussion of the Darwinian Theory of Evolution and Natural Selection or the Big Bang

"Atheists, I can put up with. It's those dog gone wishy - washy Agnostics I can't stand!"

theory should not undermine religious belief. Just because we, as a species, have grown in our understanding of the universe does not mean we have outgrown God. There are enough clues in the Bible to allow all of us not only to be comfortable with expanding our knowledge, but with expanding our faith. 🌿

CHAPTER EIGHT
GOD IS ALIVE AND GOOGLING

The Divine Search Engine

Richard Dawkins, the brilliant scientist/atheist, writes the following on page 185 of his best-selling book *The God Delusion*:

"To suggest that the original prime mover was complicated enough to indulge in intelligent design, to say nothing of mind-reading millions of humans simultaneously, is tantamount to dealing yourself a perfect hand of bridge...

"To suggest that the first cause, the great unknown... is being capable of designing the universe and of talking to a million people simultaneously is a total abdication of the responsibility to find an explanation. It is a dreadful exhibition of self-indulgent, thought-denying skyhookery."

Well, I have a surprise for Mr. Dawkins. Believe it or not, science and technology prove that God can listen to millions of prayers simultaneously and answer each and every one of them. Human scientists and engineers devised the search engine (e.g., Google) on the Internet so that millions of people can ask questions at the same time and get instant responses. If humans, with their limited

abilities, can accomplish such a feat, then surely God could do a much better job of setting up a system designed to automatically answer everybody's prayers. After installing the program, in fact,

He might even choose to move on to other planets or maybe another universe or two. He's God, after all.

Richard Dawkins has two main problems regarding God. We resolved one with this gigantic search engine. But that leaves us with the other problem: intelligent design. The theist defends God by showing organs of the body with what is termed "irreducible complexity," such as the eye or the wing. The argument put forth is that the eye can't see with one part missing, so it cannot have evolved from a lesser or more primitive eye. The same principle is true for the wing, which can't fly if one part is missing. Nor can it have evolved from a lesser wing. There are no useful intermediates. However, contrary to these long-held theories, biologists recently proved that the eye and the wing could, in fact, have evolved. So much for long-held theories.

Creationists constantly concern themselves with Darwin's theory of evolution because they believe that it contradicts the literal meaning of the Bible. Interpreting the Good Book literally shows tremendous loyalty and love for the Bible, which is admirable, but when we love something unconditionally, we tend to go to extremes, and beyond all reason, to defend it. This is true of literal interpretation, which runs contrary to common sense, when we again consider the age of the Bible, the language in which it was written, and the people for whom it was meant to appeal.

Because of scientific research, we have good reason to believe the earth is billions of years old, and not the mere 6,000 years as fundamentalists conclude from the Bible. Certainly, archeological excavations have discovered communities older than 6,000 years. However, we might agree that the Bible is correct in stating that God made man from the dust of the earth. What is not mentioned in Genesis is that it took approximately five billion years for humans to fully develop from that dust.

A parable is told by creationists that 1,000 years from

now a group of scientists will have discovered the secrets for creating a human being from dust. They go to God and say to him: "We don't need you anymore. We can make a human just as effectively as you can."

God smiles and says, "Okay. Let's see you do it."

The scientists go about gathering the dust and starting to work.

God lifts His voice and stops them in their tracks: "Hey," he muses. "That's my dust you're using. Go make your own!"

This story tells us that defenders of the Bible do not have to look for gaps in evolution or irreducible complexity to argue in favor of intelligent design. For their proof, they need only to go to the source, which is the earth. This is the biggest gap of all, since it's the starting point for Darwin's theory, in which he explains how life evolved from the earth, but does not take into account how the earth was created. If creationists and other defenders of the Bible concentrate on this gap they can readily accept evolution. Doing so would save them the time and money they usually spend fighting for their cause and trying to introduce intelligent design into schools. They must realize that science will eventually prevail and disprove their claims. So, while the gaps are bound to disappear, there is one that is likely to linger indefinitely, which is the creation of the earth and/or the universe. This is the remaining issue through which creationists will be able to defend their cause into the future.

Why does the clash persist between scientist/atheists and people of faith, who represent more than 95% of the U.S. population?

In every generation there are what I call "The Passionate Few." These are the highly intelligent people who are interested in the world, the environment, and the betterment of mankind. They pursue the major intellectual endeavors, such as: science, technology,

medicine, philosophy, and religion. Because of their innovative thinking and productivity, we have access to computers, automobiles, air travel, advanced medical procedures, psychology, and a multitude of other benefits that enhance our lifestyles, improve our health, and prolong our lives. The rest of the population simply benefits from the efforts of these Passionate Few, which allows them to drive fancy cars, watch TV, and discuss matters of the universe, without knowing what makes any of these things work. Doesn't it blow your mind to consider how insignificant we are in the scheme of things? How infinitesimal the earth is, suspended in space, and surrounded by other galaxies—other universes?

When the Scriptures were written, everybody thought that the earth was flat and the only world in existence. God had created the stars in the sky and the moon and the sun, all to serve the earth and its human race. The Bible made a lot of sense back then, even to the Passionate Few, who nonetheless kept investigating the world and slowly became responsible for expanding our knowledge. In the process, the earth, which had previously been regarded as a vast universe unto itself was seen as one small part of the infinitesimal whole. Along the way, God was promoted from local deity to master ruler of a vast, virtually boundless universe.

In terms of religious beliefs the Passionate Few are now divided into two major groups: 1) atheists/agnostics, and 2) theists/deists (the distinction being that theists believe in a personal God, whereas deists do not).

The primary reason that many scientists are atheists is that they use science to discredit the Scriptures, making it an easy win for their team. Ultimately, of course, this is an unfair competition since science is continually updated, but the Bible/religious doctrine remains static. Some scientists become deists so they don't have to accept a personal God, which defies their intellect. Perhaps, after reading this book, they may change their minds. Because the majority of us acquire very little knowledge of the universe or advance ideas of any significance throughout our lifetime, it is easy to continue following the beliefs of our ancestors, albeit with some accommodations for the material world in which we all live. ✍

✍ But the main reason almost everyone wants to believe is because it gives us a sense of purpose and security and the promise of afterlife. Atheism, by contrast, is a huge letdown. The scientists who write anti-religious books are doing a great disservice to laypeople. When they convince them that there is no God or that prayer doesn't work, they unjustly take away their irreplaceable security blanket, and yet gain nothing in return. Instead, they should stick to writing professional—not necessarily popular—books and preach to their own, secular, choir. ✍

✍ As we mentioned above, scientists/atheists are divided into two groups: 1) those who don't believe in a personal God but do believe in a creator God, and 2) those who don't believe in the existence of God. Since it does not look promising in the foreseeable future for science to prove or disprove God's existence, the only way I can suggest is an indirect route. This book postulates that God can answer all prayers using a system similar to a gigantic search engine. If my theory is correct, all we have to do is devise an elaborate scientific search to determine if, in fact, God does answer many of our prayers. In conducting this study, assuming they qualify the prayers very judiciously, science can safely assume at least a 50% positive response rate.

The Templeton group did perform this test, but not as effectively as they might have done. My own experience has been extremely positive. However, I pray very seldom. I do thank God daily for everything I have, but I rarely ask for anything. The only time I pray for something extra is when it is extremely important or when I feel desperate. So far these urgent prayers have been fulfilled each time, as I discuss in the next chapter.

What I propose is that a group of scientists first research those people who claim that their prayers have been answered satisfactorily. They could classify these cases and statistically check for results. After accumulating an abundance of information, these same scientists should then launch a comprehensive study to prove or disprove those results. If the research proves that a significant number of prayers were actually answered beyond reasonable doubt, such data would go a long way toward proving the existence of God.

A project of this kind would have an enormous impact on the world's three major religions. It would not only generate a great deal of initial interest, but were it to prove successful, it would also be celebrated by the entire world, and for a long time thereafter. It doesn't even have to be 100% successful in its findings. If the results were to show that there is more than a 50% chance that these prayers were indeed answered, that would close the argument for most skeptics.

CHAPTER NINE
MY PERSONAL
EXPERIENCE WITH PRAYER

My Prayer for Love

Sea green eyes fringed with thick, dark lashes stared down at me through a grayish haze. Faint traces of Chanel #5, drugstore lipstick, and fresh herbal shampoo filled my nostrils. Coming into focus now was the smiling face of an angel with porcelain skin and perfectly chiseled features. Atop this glorious vision's mane of shoulder-length blonde hair sat a pristine halo-like white cap. Noticing I was awake, the figure pulled away to allow me a better view, but never released my hand from her gentle grasp. For all I knew, this was the regal and beautiful Princess Grace of Monaco, herself, come to nurse me back to health in my hour of need. I smiled my silent thanks to her and to God, then slipped back into a coma.

Hours later, I had regained a level of consciousness, and grown somewhat aware of my unfamiliar surroundings—a sterile mint green room, and no sign of life other than my own steady breathing. But, where was my angel? Was she even real? Had I been dreaming? Hallucinating? I needed to know. Gradually, I came to realize that I was in a hospital bed, and I began to reconstruct the events leading up to that moment.

It was a rainy Thanksgiving just after midnight in 1955, and I was driving Polaski Skyway home to Newark, New Jersey. I had only minutes before left the Manhattan townhouse of some well-meaning friends who had stuffed me with a succulent turkey dinner, then imposed on me a thoroughly distasteful blind date whose phone number

I had already discarded. There I was in the aftermath, making my way across the slick, dark streets, wishing I were already home in bed. Blinding headlights suddenly exploded my line of vision, and a split second later, I went skidding across the ice, swerving into the opposite lane, and colliding into another vehicle—head-on.

Flashing lights. Screeching brakes. Crashing sounds. Sirens in the distance. Sensory overload in one brain-busting rush. Finally, filtered darkness. Silence. Nothing. And there she was, sitting by my side in that sickly green room, pumping up the tightening armband that measured my soaring blood pressure. My hand searched for hers and found it immediately. I wanted never to let it go. This time, I would gather the strength to stay awake, no matter what.

"How are you feeling?" she asked in her soft angelic voice.

As I opened my cotton dry mouth to respond, she inserted a glassy thermometer and took that opportunity to deliver the bad news. I had suffered a concussion and miscellaneous other injuries, and would be hospitalized for weeks. Instead of displeasure upon hearing her news, I was overjoyed at the chance to become better acquainted with her. In fact, there was no way I was going to get well enough to leave this place until I had pled my case for her hand in marriage. Yes, I was immediately that besotted.

Her name was Arlene, she told me, and all I wanted to do was roll the sound of it around in my head. Arlene! What name was ever more melodic than that? Sensations of it were already vibrating throughout my body like high voltage electricity, igniting me with the power of love.

"You'll be long asleep by the time I come back, Michael."

Never had my own name sounded so commanding as it had in her gentle keeping. Michael. Better yet, Michael and Arlene. I was grinning from ear to ear. Suddenly, a cool touch to my forehead, a whoosh of crisp white cotton, and she was headed for the door. By the time it closed behind her, I was being transported back to the gray haze of my unconscious, and far beyond.

The ins and outs of my waking state dictated the next 24 hours of my life. Once detachment was replaced with a sustained presence of being, I became a man obsessed with a woman—the goddess Arlene.

First on my agenda was to find out more about her from other nurses on the ninth floor. Devastated to learn that she was stationed on the seventh, I was reenergized thereafter by news of her transfer to the ninth. On that pronouncement alone, my hopes catapulted through the roof—having allowed myself to believe she had requested transfer to be near me.

Hospital stays can be dreary when there's nothing to look forward to except for getting back to your former existence, which, as good as mine had been, was nowhere near the heights of spectacular I was now planning to reach.

Naptime was my favorite because it allowed me to visit the most romantic places on earth that my mind could conjure. I was particularly partial to poolside at the Fontainebleau Hotel on Miami Beach, where I soaked in the tropical sun, and sipped on a mango iced tea. Seated in the lounge chair beside me was a well-formed blonde in a black bikini and white nurse's cap. Heaven itself had nothing on this place.

Waking up from my paradise was never easy, as it was usually the result of severe pain in my butt from too much down time in one position. It only added to my dismay that a broad-shouldered army nurse with Marlboro breath was now blowing words in my face. She wanted to know if I was comfortable.

"I was," I said, ironically, as she grunted, took my pulse, and propped me up for a feeding. Dinner was comprised of a distasteful selection of bouillon, hot tea, an overly poached egg, and green gelatin. I reluctantly sipped the soup, pretending it was a cheeseburger, seasoned with spicy mustard and, garnished with fresh sliced tomato. All this would have been tolerable, but for the absence of Arlene.

"Don't hurry back," I thought to myself as the hatchet-faced nurse exited the room, leaving me alone with my obsessive yearnings.

I wasted no time falling back to sleep and into the arms of the Fontainebleau blonde. Soon I was hearing her gentle voice, and when I opened my lids, I was looking into those sea green eyes and Grace Kelly smile of my nursing angel.

As Arlene took hold of my hand, I could feel my body surge with the energy of rebirth.

"Good boy," she said without sarcasm. "You've all but cleaned your plate."

To fulfill her expectations, I gulped down the remaining gelatin like the good boy she said I was, and fully expected a pat on the head.

Arlene and I spent the following days becoming better acquainted. She captivated me with stories of her typical American youth and tragicomic observations of a pretty young nurse in a bustling city hospital. I impressed her, as well, I thought, with exotic stories of my childhood in Jerusalem and military heroics that had literally set the stage for the birth of the State of Israel. Our natural chemistry was increasingly heightened by our growing respect for each other. Eventually, I told her about my job as an electrical engineer with Weston Electrical Instrument in Newark, and elaborated on my ambitious plans for the future. *Our* future, I thought to myself. ✐

✐ As my body was healing, I grew increasingly curious about the driver who had hit me on Thanksgiving night. Arlene investigated, and found out that while he had gotten off without a scratch that was more than could be said for his brand new Cadillac or my crumbled Chevy.

One particular day, just as I thought I was taking back control of my life, an off-duty nurse confided in me that I had been dreaming out loud—verbalizing passionate affirmations of love for Arlene that rang through the corridors of the ninth floor, alerting the entire staff to my romantic intentions. Fully aware of my sentiments, Arlene continued to maintain a professional silence about her feelings toward me. Finally, one day, when I was fully conscious, she broke the news for which I was completely unprepared. For the past three years, she had been seeing a somewhat older man named Howard, and finally accepted his proposal of marriage. As evidence, she removed her left hand from her pocket, and shone a diamond dazzler in my eyes. Howard was an impressive man, as Arlene described him. He was a successful attorney residing in a high-end Manhattan penthouse overlooking the East River, and reveled in his habit of spoiling her rotten. I quickly compared Howard's credentials to my own pathetic $80 a week salary at Weston Electric and the tiny space in New Jersey I could barely call home. There was no way for me to compete with this man based on our material qualifications, and I was devastated at the likelihood that I had met the love of my life only to be doomed to her loss.

Seeing the desolation written across my painful expression, Arlene apologized profusely for having unintentionally misled me. She had certainly not meant to hurt my feelings. But once she left the room, my mind raced into overdrive, bent on creating a scenario in which I could win Arlene away from her seemingly suitable match. In the process, I managed to convince myself that the only reason she was marrying him was that she had met him first, dated him for three years, and was far too honorable to break his heart after all this time. I also suspected her parents approved of him whole-heartedly, and had even encouraged the relationship from the beginning. After all, in accordance with parental guidelines, Howard had all the qualities any young woman would be lucky to find in a husband. On the surface, the facts were undeniable. I was going to have to dig way deeper than that. ∅

❂ In the green setting of my solitude, the ticking clock struck away at my youthful longings, and diminished me to a simpering sop. I was only 24 years old, and suddenly finding myself at a bigger turning point than I felt emotionally capable of handling. In spite of my flimsy chances, I was compelled to follow my passion, as it was obvious to me Arlene was the one woman on earth that was born to share my life. Now that I had found her, I could not see beyond the tomorrow that would take her away from me. Although my body was hardly up to the task, my brain was in perfect focus. I took its advice, and did what it commanded of me. Pray, like there was no tomorrow. ❂

I lay there for what seemed like hours. My mind filled with images of the life I had not yet lived with Arlene — but hoped to, with all my heart. As clear as if it were happening at that precise moment in time, I saw Arlene enter my hospital room the next morning. Her left ring finger was absent of the diamond rock. She told me she had broken her engagement to Howard — that she realized she did not love him, and could not, therefore, marry him.

I saw myself so overjoyed that I hugged her for a very long time, and she hugged me back with equal fervor. The scenario progressed effortlessly thereafter, and I observed in delight as I courted her — first from the hospital bed, then, on the outside. There were simple dinners at home, walks in the park, and the gushy proposal at a candlelit restaurant, where, on bended knee, I declared my love, surrounded by a roomful of cheering strangers. After that, I saw the wedding play out with all the family present. Best of all, I saw us making love on the most romantic wedding night my imagination could conjure — roaring fireplace, rain on the roof, rose petals strewn on soft silk sheets across an oversized bed, and our hearts bursting with love for each other as we expressed it in physical terms. And there was more. I saw us buying a small starter house, then a larger one. I saw my career increasingly successful. I saw Arlene give birth to our children, one by one. I saw myself playing with my kids, taking them to school, taking care of them when they were sick, applauding their every accomplishment. Life as I saw it was perfect because it was filled with Arlene and all that we had created together.

My heart was racing as I silently spelled it all out to God in the most heartfelt of terms. Not only was I praying out of desperation, but also because I knew that in marrying me, Arlene would have found the deepest measure of happiness she could find with a mate in this lifetime.

"Please, God," I thought. *"I am not a praying man, but I know you are an intelligent being, and I also know you would not be bringing this incredible woman into my life in the way you did only to let her slip away from me forever. I'll do anything to have Arlene for my wife. I'll devote the rest of my life to making her happy. I'll buy her not just one penthouse, but two, maybe three—and bigger and better than Howard's. I believe beyond doubt that Arlene and I were born to love and be loved by each other, and if what I believe is true by your preeminent standards, I ask you to make it possible for us to be together in the way that I envision. If you choose to answer my prayer, I will do anything you ask of me as long as I live. I would even be willing to attend synagogue regularly. I swear this to you, God. Amen."*

I do not know how long the process of that prayer took in terms of real time. I only know that I lived out a lifetime in the course of communicating it to God. When it was over, it came to me that if Arlene were not wearing her engagement ring the following morning when she came into my room, it was an indisputable sign from God that he had heard my prayer, and was answering it. I fell asleep in the certainty of that message.

The next morning, I woke up to Arlene's fresh scent. She smiled down at me as she inserted the glass thermometer in my mouth with her left hand. I swallowed hard at the sight of her suddenly naked ring finger. It happened, just as

I knew it would. God had given me his stamp of approval, and was sending me a clear message to that effect. I tried to contain my euphoria. When I asked Arlene about the missing ring, the answer was more complicated and more challenging than I had anticipated.

"It was too big and it kept falling off my finger. I had to take it back to the jeweler for resizing," she said.

After the initial blow, I reassessed the situation, and interpreted it to mean that while God was prepared to answer my prayer, he was demanding I prove myself worthy and sincere. It made perfect sense to me.

That night, as the snow obscured the city view from my window, I had a long talk with myself, knowing that God was listening. I said, "*If I have acquired any wisdom in life so far, it's that God helps those who help themselves. I can either allow the situation to play out as written—Arlene riding off into the sunset with the wrong guy—or I can do the proactive thing, and prove myself to be the better man, which I am already convinced that I am.*" I chose to follow God's plan, which he had already set in place for me. ♪

♪ Courting Arlene from my hospital bed, I found the results no less than miraculous. Somehow, my physically challenged charm had so overwhelmed her that by the holidays, despite her engagement to Howard, she chose to celebrate with me in my hospital room instead of with him in a chic Manhattan bistro. I could see God pulling for me every step of the way.

Proof came the day Arlene broke her engagement to Howard, which was just two weeks after I left the hospital. She said she realized she wanted to see in the New Year with me—and all of our new years to come. Only three months after we met, Arlene and I were married. Our lives together thereafter followed the precise pattern I had envisioned in my impassioned plea.

Ultimately, God had listened, observed, and answered my prayer for love. ♪

MY PRAYER FOR LIVELIHOOD

Early in my adult life I learned that if you are going to work for a living you might as well labor at the thing you love most. Coincidentally, what you love is generally what you do best. In my case, that principle worked nearly perfectly for decades, as I acquired and developed increasing numbers of commercial and residential property—first in New York, then in California, and finally, in Nevada. The more years and money I invested in my career, the better I became at finding and developing the finest properties at the right time, and turning them over for a substantial profit.

Because the real estate industry is cyclical, there's more to the business than buying and selling; there's that unique skill in knowing when to hold onto a property and when to let it go—and at what price. Over the years, I honed that skill to the degree that it had worked for me upwards of 90% of the time. When you are accurate in assessing the big picture, you do exceedingly well. But you must never forget that investing in real estate is like playing poker in Las Vegas: the house is against your every move, and will likely catch up with you somewhere along the way, no matter how good you are at what you are doing. Ironically, it was in Las Vegas for me where a group of houses almost took me down—and yet not quite. Was it the luck of the draw that allowed me to prevail? Was it coincidence? Was it prayer? There is no doubt in my mind it was the prayer. When I reveal the facts as they played out, you would find it difficult to believe otherwise.

If you happened to read a newspaper, watch TV, browse the Internet, or were paying off a mortgage in 2008, you could not avoid keeping up with the news about the nationwide housing crisis. Homes by the thousands had fallen into foreclosure. Banks big and small had gone bankrupt. Seemingly overnight, the overheated real estate market descended into a new Ice Age, as the money supply dried up and easy credit went into deep freeze.

No one is infallible. Sometimes it takes a crisis of epic proportions to discover that about yourself. With the real estate market in Las Vegas and surrounding area literally on fire, David and I had miscalculated the risk of a downturn, and we built the wrong houses in the wrong area at exactly the wrong time.

About five years ago, when the markets were still looking robust in Nevada, David became particularly excited about a piece of land in Henderson, about ten miles outside of Las Vegas. It was not a desirable location, as it faced a rundown commercial area, but with the whole region in growth mode, it nonetheless appeared a sound investment.

I was not available when the papers were drawn, so, in his excitement, David went out on a limb and signed a personal note for $1.9 million, which rendered him extremely vulnerable.

We called the property Palm Eight, because it was located on Palm Street and also because it was designed to accommodate eight separate properties. After inspecting the land, I told David I thought it was big enough to take three more lots than we had anticipated, so we changed the name to Palm Eleven. In spite of our new commitment, I remained reluctant to build anything on the land, as I didn't think it offered sufficient appeal to homebuyers. With mounting pressure from David, however, I agreed to begin construction, but only, at first, for six of the eleven homes.

In order to build the houses, we hired a contractor, who recommended we build all eleven at once, as it would be more cost effective, and the market was strong. In his enthusiasm, he assured us the houses would sell like hotcakes. Ironically, a few months later, just as the project was completed, the market began to collapse, and so did our hopes for repaying our debt.

Because of my knowledge of the markets, I had long ago found a system to keep myself afloat during down cycles—it required simply that I be free of debt. Before this debacle took place, David and I had raised $45 million from investors, and, as a result, owned $100 million in debt-free property. I made particularly sure we owned everything outright, because I knew that this unrealistically extended cycle would eventually turn against us, and the worst thing an investor can do in a down cycle is owe money on property that is not producing income. It's the surest way to lose your assets, and it was how many Americans began losing theirs in 2008, even some of the largest corporations led by some of the most seemingly astute investors. Stock in the Sheldon Adelson-run Venetian Hotel plummeted from $146 a share to $6 in early November. MGM went from $96 to $10. As the end of the year approached, the skyline of Las Vegas was still alive with cranes, primarily as remnants of the building boom that had not yet burned to the ground.

My one mistake, and it was huge, was those eleven new homes in Henderson, propped up in an undesirable setting and wanting desperately to be bought and lived in.

The view from eight of the lots was particularly bleak. You would see a major wall called The Highway, which is a secondary Strip and home to the dilapidated but familiar landmark called Sam's Town. Rows of old casinos and rundown hotels from a bygone era of low-rise commercial structures filled your line of vision. Because of this unsightly spectacle, the eight homes looking out on it were going to be the toughest sell—and yet, ironically, those were the first to go.

The selling phase began with Diana, a broker David and I had met in Las Vegas. In order to arrive at a fair price for the homes, she suggested we hire an appraiser, who took note of the many innovations we had installed in the houses, and came up with the lofty value of $350,000—far in excess of the $230,000-250,000 range we had been considering. Diana was thrilled at the elevated price, which she saw as a way to leverage potential buyers. Out of the $350,000, we would pay her commission, and she would hold back between $20,000 and $30,000 as carrots to offer the buyer.

With confidence in her new strategy, Diana held her first open house. Nothing sold. Then, suddenly a man who worked across the street in the commercial area bought one of the homes because of the convenience to his business. Over the coming weeks, the market spiraled steadily downward. Out of desperation, Diana came up with the idea of selling the homes to buyers in Los Angeles who could, in turn, rent them out and provide them with income. Her idea turned out to be inspired, because over the course of the next six or seven months, she managed to sell all eight of those houses. She was so excited by her success that she tried to convince us to build twenty more houses, assuring us she could sell every one. Then the market collapsed with gusto, and that put an end to that idea. But the news was generally good. With the profits that came from the last sale, David and I were able to pay off the mortgage to the Silver State Bank. As for the three other homes, we rented out two, and agreed to sell the last one at the reduced price of $180,000.

Prayer was a more complex matter in this story, as neither David nor I confided in the other about the fact that we had begun praying to God individually, and on an ongoing basis. Desperation had taken hold of each of us from the moment of the market downtown, and neither was willing to share the depths of our concerns until the crisis had passed, and we were back on safe financial ground. Only then did we admit to each other what we had done, convinced as we both were that our prayers to God had been answered.

by Michael Bash

^o What gives this story such a sense of the miraculous is the following:

We were able to sell eight of the houses at the same high price, regardless of their location and the fact that the market was in a tailspin.

Anyone could have gone half a mile away and bought beautiful homes in a gated community, comparable to the more upscale area in which I lived. David and I discovered there were bigger and more luxurious homes than the ones we had built, and they were on the market for $200,000 at the same time our inferior ones were selling for $350,000. Why would anyone looking for a house to buy not first have checked the classifieds, compared prices and amenities, and chosen the better deal? Why would they intentionally have chosen to buy a home of lesser value and in a less desirable area? And yet they did.

After we paid off our mortgage to them, the Silver State Bank went bankrupt and was thereafter taken over by the FDIC.

In a desperate attempt to stay afloat, our building contractor who was invested elsewhere in million-dollar-plus homes that were heavily mortgaged at between $30 and $40 million, borrowed against his secretary's house (which she lost as a result), and invariably was forced into bankruptcy.

In the new hostile environment, Diana, the broker, had no alternative but to scale down her business, and is now working out of her home.

Two or three of the homes that we sold soon after went into foreclosure. Those who were able to keep the homes they bought from David and me lost nearly 50% of their value.

In my own series of prayers to God on the subject of this grave financial crisis in Henderson, I followed my tested formula, hoping to be successful once again in gaining God's favor. I knew that the consequences would

61

be horrendous if we were not able to sell enough of the houses to pay off the mortgage and gain sufficient profit, at least, to sustain us for a while. By this time, there were virtually no loans to be had from the banks, no matter how pristine your credit, or how enormous your debt-free inventory of property. Institutions of lending were now being closed down and bought up by one another at a frenetic pace. There were no available seats for outsiders on this financial merry-go-round.

This time around, my prayer session did not stop at one, but continued routinely and yet spontaneously from the day I learned the seriousness of our situation. In my mind, I began envisioning each one of the homes being sold at market value. I saw myself at the bank with David paying off our mortgage in full. I saw some measure of profit, enough to sustain us through the rough period that followed. In the process, I reminded God that I had many people depending on me for support on various levels, both personal and professional—and in helping me survive, He would be helping them, as well.

While most parties to our enterprise failed miserably during the downturn, David and I were left not only unscathed, but also in profit.

Although David prays on any subject on a daily basis, and in accordance with his religious beliefs, thus far I had only prayed in times of personal crisis, or if I were to see myself on a particularly shaky brink of potential ruin. In this case, David was so concerned with looming calamity that he not only prepared special prayers for himself to conduct, he resorted to extreme measures by approaching two famous rabbis in Israel (reputed to be "magical") and asked them, too, to pray for our success. He was leaving no spiritual stone unturned. Soon after his mother died— assuming she now enjoyed a closer relationship with God than he did— he prayed to her to help him out in any way she might be able to arrange, given her new set of circumstances.

As a tradition, David and I give a certain portion of profit from any and all of our income to charitable—generally Jewish—causes. We made no exception in this case. David combined special tithing in combination with his prayers, and I tithed, as well.

In the end, I realized that although God had helped us, it was in part at the expense of others. There was no way to explain away what seemed to me an injustice. I can only conclude from what took place that as human beings we go through life, and rather than get what we want, we are often given what we need. In this case, there was a harsh lesson to be learned in terms of fiscal responsibility. As expensive a lesson as it turned out to be, I hope it was so well learned by those who were faced with it, that it will never be forgotten or repeated.

While the love and life of others are the two most important extensions of our own lives, livelihood is essential to the quality of both—often dictating everything we do. In this second and extraordinary example of prayer at work, God heard my plea in concert with that of David—and sustained our lives and livelihood for yet another day.

Why me? 🖉

🖉 In reviewing this book, Harold Kushner, who wrote the classic bestseller, *Why Bad Things Happen to Good People* asked me, "How do you think a reader who lost a child would feel when he or she sees that God answered your prayer to change Arlene's mind and break her engagement to someone else to marry you? He or she had a prayer about a much more serious matter, and, while their prayer was not answered, yours was."

MY UNANSWERED PRAYER FOR REVIVAL

am a fortunate man. God has answered some of my most fervent prayers. But, as you are about to find out, the most heartfelt prayer of my entire life was ultimately disregarded.

It was Thanksgiving Day. Our family had just finished our traditional turkey dinner with all the trimmings. Arlene and I were seated on the living room sofa watching TV with daughter Sharon. Son Joel was reading a book at the kitchen table.

Suddenly, Arlene fell to the floor and stopped breathing. It was a heart attack. I yelled to Joel to call 911, then immediately tried to revive my wife. Her mouth was clenched tight, so I tried to pry it open with a spoon, and, in the process, I broke one or two of her teeth. By that time, the paramedics had arrived, and attempted to resuscitate her while transporting her into the ambulance.

I got into my car and followed the ambulance to the nearby hospital, where I was told that it took the rescue crew twenty minutes to revive my wife, but since her brain had been deprived of oxygen for that period of time, it was showing no signs of activity. Essentially, my wife was alive, but her brain was not.

An Indian doctor came to me and assured me that Arlene had no chance of recovery. That her brain was dead, and such a condition offered not a glimmer of hope for revival. I chose not to believe him. Instead, I called the head of Cedars-Sinai Hospital, with whom I was acquainted. He arranged that a bed be made available for Arlene on the prestigious eighth floor, where celebrities go to get well, or not. In fact, Arlene's next-door neighbor was legendary actress, Lucille Ball.

For Arlene's primary physician, I chose the head of

the cardiac unit. Two additional doctors were also put in her charge. After interviewing fifteen nurses, I chose the best three for round-the-clock care. I was satisfied that her medical team would be first-rate.

Every one of the doctors told me, individually, that Arlene had no chance of revival, that her brain was dead, and that was, essentially, that. And yet I persisted in my futile quest for her recovery. With youngest son Jeremy for company, every day of the week I remained by my wife's side, from eight in the morning until midnight. Together, Jeremy and I prayed for Arlene.

After a while, I arranged for the visit of the Chief Rabbi of Israel, Rabbi Eliahu, who came to pray for her. Rabbi Pinto, a self-described miracle worker from France, arrived, spent an hour with her, and announced to me, "She will get up and live." I chose to believe him. There was also a minister from a local church who came and placed oil on her head, and prayed for a very long time. But, of course, nothing worked.

Despite the hopeless prognosis, Arlene lay in her hospital bed looking beautiful, well groomed, and staring blankly at the ceiling above her. One day when I was there with one of the nurses, Arlene opened her mouth, and said, "It's wonderful. I am fine. Thank God." She continued her monologue, but her words were incoherent. Excited by the new development, I called in a friend who worked in post-production. He rushed in and shot close-up film of Arlene moving her lips, but in speech that was unintelligible. Determined to crack the code of Arlene's mumblings, I hired an expert from a school for the deaf, hoping he would be able to read her lips. But to no avail.

After that, I began talking to her at great length, hoping the familiarity of my voice would stir something in her to speak more coherently. Again, without success. Then I came up with an idea to entertain her. I began saying funny things, making silly faces and gestures. Surprisingly, she smiled, even laughed. I was encouraged enough to call in all three of her doctors and demonstrate how she was reacting to my attempts at humor. They investigated the phenomenon and concluded that while her primitive brain was still alive and reacting to my jokes, her cerebrum, her upper brain, was dead and beyond repair. To illustrate, one doctor compared the death of a brain with the loss a finger. In neither case can there be regeneration.

And still I refused to give up. I prayed to God, telling him: "God, you gave me this woman twenty-eight years ago. Why have you taken her away now, when she's only forty-nine? She is a wonderful woman, and doesn't deserve such an untimely end. Nor does our family deserve the loss of this beautiful, sweet, generous, and giving woman."

Against all advice to the contrary, my attitude remained hopeful. Somehow Arlene would defy the odds and come back to me. Once again, I called Rabbi Pinto to return, which he did. As he walked around her bed, Arlene followed him with her eyes. "You see?" he said to me. "She knows I'm here. She will be revived." Before leaving, he scribbled some undecipherable writings across the walls and around her bed.

I kept up this practice for some time. Friends and family would visit and try to calm me. My father came in from Israel to celebrate Passover, which we did in Arlene's hospital room. Before he left, he turned to me and said: "I never ordered you to do anything in your life, but I'm doing it now. Give up on her. Can't you see by now there is no hope? If you continue doing what you've been doing, it will ruin your life!"

But I ignored my father's pleas, and, along with Jeremy, continued my routine of prayer.

Finally, after an emotional wrenching two and a half years, I gave up. I stopped visiting the hospital every day, and Arlene contracted pneumonia and passed on. In a way, I believe, I gave her permission to die.

So, although God had answered my prayers in the past, this time, he could not. The laws of physics dictate that a dead brain cannot be revived. Intellectually, I knew that to be true, but emotionally I had a much more difficult time. I now realize that even God cannot change the laws of the universe.

Recently, the East Coast of the United States was hit by a super-storm called Sandy. The devastation resulted in a great deal of suffering. One woman lost her two small children, when they were wrenched from her grasp by the surging waters. Flooding enveloped the coastal regions. There was great loss of life and property. God was unable to prevent this from happening. There is no perfect world. And there is no perfect God.

After my wife's death, I had strange encounters, which seemed to hint of an afterlife. It was December 19th, about a year following her passing. I was awakened in the middle of the night and went to the bathroom. When I returned, I noticed that Arlene's portrait, the one I had painted, was missing from the wall in front of me. On closer inspection, I noticed it had separated from the wall and then apparently slipped to the floor behind the dresser. It must have been the noise from the fall that awakened me. Instinctively, I looked at my watch. It was fifteen minutes after midnight on December 20th. Arlene's birthday. Her way of making sure I would not forget her special day.

When I moved Arlene to Cedars-Sinai a few years before, I purchased five condos in a building nearby, which was conveniently close to the hospital. One unit was for me, and the other four were for each of my four children. One day I received notice from the management to remove everything I had in the storage room, which was for reasons of safety, as the heating system was located there, along with the furnace. The following Thursday morning, a Salvation Army truck was scheduled to come by and pick up whatever was left behind. I went into the storage room and found several of Arlene's handbags and hundreds of books. As instructed, I removed everything I wanted to keep, and left the rest for the Salvation Army.

On Thursday morning, I realized I was missing a book that held special significance for me. In grade school, I had been the editor of the monthly newspaper, and accumulated all the issues that were published during my tenure. Years later, I had them all bound in a single volume. The book held great memories for me. And I had inadvertently left it in the storage room. I rushed downstairs, hoping to salvage it, but the truck had come and gone, along with my book. Hoping it was not too late, I ran outside, and saw the truck about three blocks in the distance. Just as I was ready to give up any thoughts of seeing it again, I stumbled on a large book in the street. My book. Out of hundreds of books that had made their way onto the truck, it was this book alone that refused to go along for the ride. I could see the hand of Arlene all over this incident. She's really never left me at all.

And that was not the only time she made her presence known to me in the intervening years. I recall how much Arlene loved diamonds. And I loved Arlene. So, over the course of our marriage, I showered her with a variety of the precious gemstones, the largest of which was an 18-carat Marquise-cut diamond ring. But her favorite jewelry of all was a pair of 5-carat diamond studs, which she wore nearly every day. Following the attack, and before she was taken to the hospital, I removed the earrings and a diamond necklace she was wearing. In my hazy recollection of that event, I thought I had given them to my son Joel for safekeeping. A couple of years later, after Arlene passed away, I asked Joel to take the diamonds out of the safe and return them to me. After looking in his safe, he told me he could not find them. In fact, he did not even remember my giving them to him.

Twelve years later, my daughter was getting married.

The day before the wedding, I was in my wardrobe closet and discovered a particular old suit hanging in there that I thought I had long since given it away. Searching the pockets, I had a bigger surprise. One of the pockets contained a pouch. And the pouch, as it turned out, contained the missing earrings and necklace. In my mind, all I could think was, *Arlene wanted me to give these as a wedding gift to our daughter.*

When I presented Sharon with her mother's cherished gems, she was amazed and delighted. Yet another indication that, while Arlene was gone, she hadn't ever left. How else to explain how her jewelry was hidden in my closet for all those years, and found exactly one day before our daughter's wedding?

Sometimes prayers are answered but in ways we don't comprehend.

We assume that God is omnipotent and omniscient, and is therefore unlimited in his capacity to do anything without disturbing the basic laws of the universe. As I discuss in my later chapter on suffering, the world was created and evolves based on fixed laws that cannot be changed. For example, one plus one equals two. As much as we might try, we would not be able to make one and one equal anything else. It is therefore futile to ask God to do anything that runs counter to those laws, which includes such natural disasters as earthquakes and tsunamis as well as many devastating diseases that have thus far eluded a definitive cure.

I also believe that because God is the creator of the whole universe and we are only a tiny part of it, He answers prayers utilizing a system that bares a resemblance—albeit more complex—to an Internet search engine such as Google. However, like the mighty Google, God can only respond to information that is previously set in place and therefore compatible with the program.

To anyone seeking an answer to an urgent prayer, I

can only offer this suggestion. Serve God in ways that you would want Him to serve you, while understanding that even God's powers have limitations. And never stop expressing your gratitude. No one gets out of this world alive, as we know, so while we are here, let's strive to make it a better place. In doing so, I suspect we are answering God's most fervent prayers for the entire universe if not entirely answering our own. ❧

CHAPTER TEN
EMOTIONS IN MOTION

*All Religions Were Formed
to Teach People Moral Values*

It could be said that the late Christopher Hitchens, in his last book, *God is not Great: How Religion Poisons Everything*, demonstrated negative emotions instead of common sense. Using contemporary ideas, he criticized the Scriptures that were written thousands of years ago, and targeted religion as the root cause of wars, genocides, and various types of human suffering. By taking this extreme position, Hitchens failed to make his point!

Just as money is *not* the root of all evil, as has often been claimed, neither is religion the cause of all chaos. Rather it is what people do in the name of money or religion that is at fault. Money itself is a good thing, capable of providing freedom to live as we choose and to contribute to the welfare of others. Its possibilities are limited only by the intentions of those who possess it.

1 Timothy 6:10: *The LOVE of money is the root of all evil, not money itself.*

Money, like nuclear material, has tremendous power, but cannot decide for you how to use it. That's up to your brain. Unfortunately or otherwise your emotions control your brain. Good emotions encourage good deeds, but

bad emotions generate the reverse. The same applies to religion, which is a system of beliefs and moral laws. These beliefs are so powerful and intoxicating that they impact the community and every individual within its perimeters.

Religion, as described in Scriptures, was created for two reasons: 1) to explain the purpose of life and the creation of the universe and 2) to create law and order and promote peace and harmony. Religion, by definition—if not always in practice—possesses only good characteristics. Those individuals controlled by their negative emotions exploit religion to accomplish their self-serving goals, and, in the process, destroy innocent people and property in the name of their god.

Belief in a Creator infuses individuals with a sense of security and purpose, just as the Bible, with its compelling prose and poetry, tends to instill a sense of awe. The concept of an almighty God having created the world and thereafter looking out for His people prompts them to reach out to Him when they are in need. Christians attend church on Sundays, while Jews observe the Sabbath on Saturdays, and Muslims on Fridays. Men and women marry in their respective houses of worship. In keeping with their religious principles, Christians baptize their babies while Jews and Muslims circumcise their boys. Within a religious environment, life is structured and comfortable.

When an evil emotion ignites, everything in its wake is negatively affected, even obliterated. The evil-inclined ego dictates: "My religion is the only true religion" or "If you don't follow my religion you are an infidel and must be destroyed!"

It is well known that Jews have the largest number by far of Nobel Prize winners. Is it because they are smarter than any other religious group? No. It's because the Jewish culture and tradition promotes learning and accomplishment. On the other hand, very few athletes are Jewish. What accounts for this imbalance? It seems to begin in childhood. Even an adopted child from non-Jewish biological parents who is raised in a nurturing Jewish environment would appreciate the value of education and productivity.

In keeping with his theme in *God is not Great: How Religion Poisons Everything*, Hitchens could as easily have written a sequel entitled, *Wealth is Not Wonderful: How Money Poisons Everything* or *Love is Not Lovely: How Sex Poisons Everything* or *Success is Not Sweet: How Fame and Fortune Poison Everything*. In the same manner, Richard Dawkins, who wrote *The God Delusion*, could write several sequels of his own, such as *The Love Delusion* or *The Wealth Delusion* or *The Success Delusion*.

We can see from these examples that all the great assets available to humanity can be spoiled by emotions—the negative emotion being the true source of the poison. I can cite many examples: 1) Religious fundamentalists, many of whom are led by their emotions, argue irrationally to prove their irrational point; 2) Orthodox Jews practice strict ancient rituals three times daily; 3) Creationists spend millions of dollars defending the Bible that does not need defending,  and 4) Muslims cover their women, head to toe, and face Mecca five times daily. All this because they are influenced by their emotions rather than reasonable thought and logic.

Wealthy people who lost their money during the Great Depression reacted primarily in one of two ways: Unable to face adversity, some committed suicide by leaping from a tall building, while others survived and went on to create new wealth.

Palestinian Muslims extremists, overtaken by their emotions, are recruited as suicide bombers in the fight with Israelis over disputed land, while moderate Muslims, influenced by good emotions, work toward peace. The late Egyptian president, Anwar Sadat, achieved peace between Egypt and Israel, but was assassinated by fanatics who used religion as a basis for their actions.

The same level of negative emotions generated during childhood inspired Dawkins and Hitchens to launch their atheist crusades against God and religion. Healthy emotions, by contrast, would encourage people to retain their beliefs while respecting the rights of others to do the same.

HOW DO WE RESOLVE ALL OF THESE EMOTIONAL PROBLEMS?
THE ANSWER IS SCIENCE.

Science helps us in a variety of ways:

1) Technology develops smart, emotionless computers to make our complex decisions;

2) Psychology develops new methods of treatment for sick emotions;

3) Medical research develops substances to restore positive emotions.

I am confident that science will continue to find ways to help us live healthier and more meaningful lives, just as religion helps us on a spiritual level. Ultimately, science and religion complement each other. Science tells us how. Religion tells us why.

"You may call me an agnostic, but I do not share the crusading spirit of the professional atheist whose fervor is mostly due to a painful act of liberation from the fetters of religious indoctrination received in youth. I prefer an attitude of humility corresponding to the weakness of our intellectual understanding of nature and of our own being."

- Albert Einstein

CHAPTER ELEVEN
A CASE FOR ATHEISM?

No Proof of God?

n September 24, 2011 an article written by Jon M. Pompia entitled "No Proof of God" appeared on the Internet. It states, in part: "The renowned scientist, professor and author who popularized the phrase 'Science flies you to the moon. Religion flies you into buildings,' brought his case for atheism last week to, of all places, a local church. Victor Stenger, 76, a professor of physics at the University of Hawaii and adjunct professor of philosophy at the University of Colorado, drew about 75 listeners to the Unitarian Church of Pueblo on the East Side."

In response to Stenger's oft-quoted theme, I came up with a variation: "Religion builds hospitals. Science sends you to their emergency rooms." (The charge against science here refers to the development of gunpowder, poison gas, anthrax, and all manner of lethal chemicals and weaponry.)

Technically, neither of our phrases is correct: Stenger's or mine. It is neither religion nor science that perpetrates acts of violence. Rather it is those individuals who exploit one or the other of them for their own purposes. Every pursuit in life has its shadow side. So it is easy to manipulate that darker side beyond reason in order to convince targeted individuals and groups that the rest of the world is evil—particularly those whose belief systems conflict with our own.

Stenger tried to make "his case against the Judeo-Christian-Islamic God, and highlighted the detrimental effects he believes religion has had on both science and the progress of humanity." His scientific argument claims: "an absence of evidence [of God] is evidence of absence."

by Michael Bash

God does not believe in Atheism
therefore Atheism does not exist

One commonality between Stenger and me is that we both graduated (a year apart) from New Jersey Institute of Technology (NJIT). Where we differ, and strongly, is on the subject of religion. Unlike Stenger, I am convinced there *is* sufficient evidence of God, which has been largely ignored since His encounter with Moses on Mount Sinai and the revelation—and significance—of His name.

Despite all the multiple translations of the Bible over the eons, and even those of fundamentalist "purists," God is never called Ehyeh. He is called Jehovah, yes. Yahweh, yes. Allah, yes. Adonai, yes. Ehyeh, NO.

In our relatively enlightened 21st century, there remains controversy over whether or not God actually wrote the words that appear in Exodus. But could such a complex concept as evolution be credited to a human being of that period? If anything speaks to the existence of God, it is this immutable statement: "I will be that which I will be."

Victor Stenger's criterion for ultimately settling the debate over God's existence would be for Him to make a public appearance in physical form. Stenger decries the excuse held by the faithful that God remains hidden in order to test the faith of mankind, but does not take into consideration God's public appearance 3,300 years ago. Doesn't he keep up with the news? And despite God's appearance at Mount Sinai, still there are skeptics.

I would like to believe that if billions of us were to call out to God as Ehyeh on a daily basis (in prayers, hymns, meditations, etc.), He might consider forgiving us for ignoring His true name all these years, and, as a result, the lives of everyone on this planet could improve exponentially. It's certainly worth a try.

P.S. As an added benefit for the acceptance of an evolving God would invariably be the fundamentalist acceptance of evolution. A God that evolves means that man also evolves. Since God made mankind "forever," it seems logical to me that He knew we would catch onto his message. It was only a matter of time.

CHAPTER TWELVE
DID THE BIBLE
PREDICT 9/11?

In Genesis 12:2, God speaks to Abraham: *"I will make you into a great nation and I will bless you; I will make your name great and you will be a blessing. I will bless those who bless you and whoever curses you I will curse. And all people on earth will be blessed through you."*

This is God's eternal blessing on the Jews, and the biblical source for Christian belief that Jews are God's chosen people.

There are other stories in the Bible addressing blessings and prophecies of a particular individual prior to birth. Samuel and Jesus are prime examples. While most of these prophecies tend to be positive in nature, one is a glaring exception, and can only be viewed, particularly in light of history, as deeply foreboding.

Most of us are familiar with the Genesis 16 story of Hagar. Because Abraham's elderly wife, Sara, was unable to conceive, she gave Abraham permission to sleep with her servant, Hagar, in order to produce an offspring and fulfill God's prophesy that Abraham would become the father of many nations. When Hagar became pregnant, she began to despise Sara, who, with her husband's approval, began treating her abusively. Ultimately, Hagar fled into the desert, where an Angel of the Lord spoke to her near a spring.

The Angel made two prophecies. One begins with verse 9 and reads as follows: *Then the Angel of the Lord told her: "Go back to your mistress and submit to her. I will so increase your descendants that they will be too numerous to count."*

The second prophecy begins in verse 11: *"You are now*

*with child, and you will have a son. You shall name him Ishmael
(in Hebrew, "God will listen"), for the Lord has heard your
misery. He will be a wild donkey of a man. His hand will be
against everyone and everyone's hand against him. And he will
live in hostility toward his brothers."*

One can only wonder if this prophecy predicted the

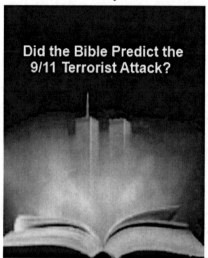

Did the Bible Predict the
9/11 Terrorist Attack?

eventual conflicts between
the Arab nations, which
began with Ishmael and
the Judeo-Christian West.
Considering that the two
predictions are stated in
verses 9 and 11, one wonders,
as well, if they might have
foretold the attacks on the
World Trade Center.

If these prophecies are
indeed to be taken as literal
truth, it begs the question,
why? Why would God
want Ishmael to fight with his brothers? Didn't He bless all
of Abraham's descendants? Wouldn't that include Ishmael?
In response to the last question, it could be argued that the
boy was not born through the will of God, but of Sara.

A similar story is told in Genesis 30:3 about Rachel's
inability to conceive with Jacob. The verse reads: *Then she
said, "Here is Billah, my maidservant. Sleep with her so that she
can bear children for me, and that through her I can build a family."*

Reminiscent of Abraham and Sara's story, Rachel's
decision led to trouble for Jacob's family. Ah, but that's a
story for another time. ❧

CHAPTER THIRTEEN
AN OPEN LETTER TO VICTOR STENGER

Author of
God, the Failed Hypothesis

Dear Vic;

a Thank you for your prompt and informative reply to my email.

In your response, you said: "I do not regard myself or the new atheists as 'fundamentalists.' Show us the evidence and we will believe." In light of your claim, you might be particularly interested to note that Webster's Dictionary assigns more than one meaning to the word *fundamentalism*: 1) Protestant religious movement emphasizing the literal infallibility of the Bible, and 2) a movement or attitude stressing strict adherence to a set of basic principles.

In attempting to distance yourself and the atheist/scientist community from accusations of fundamentalism, you have overlooked that pivotal second definition as stated above. While it is apparent that the first meaning refers primarily to "creationists," the second readily applies to atheists/scientists, who require no less than hard evidence as basis for establishing fact. And yet, the human mind is impatient for answers. While advancements in contemporary science and technology provide detailed explanations of "how" things work, our perennial questions of "why" continue to be dismissed or discredited.

In accordance with the New Testament method of confirming future events through biblical prophesy, I thought you would appreciate the following verse from Isaiah: Chapter 1, which predicts the abandonment of the Bible by the scientific community: *I have nourished and brought up children, And they have rebelled against Me; The ox knows its owner and the donkey its master's crib; But Israel does not know, My people do not consider...*

There are approximately six billion people in the world. About two billion of those are Christians, less than 15 million are Jews, one billion or more are Muslim, and the remaining three billion follow Eastern philosophies and assorted other ideologies.

The Judeo-Christian value system as presented in the Holy Bible has, over the millennia, set standards that inspired a vast majority of the scientific achievements ascribed to humankind. Without these discoveries and inventions, we might not yet enjoy our extended lifespan or those advanced technologies of the automobile, airplane, television, computer, cell phone, space travel, and atomic energy.

There is no way to dismiss the fact that nearly all Nobel Prize winners have been Christians or Jews. In fact, Jews have won considerably more Nobels than Christians, in proportion to their numbers. Albert Einstein, Sigmund Freud, and Jonas Salk immediately come to mind. Why have Jews seemed to excel more than Christians? The answer may lie in the fact that followers of Judaism "discovered" God 2,000 years before Christendom was established, and that the Hebrew Bible predates the New Testament by 1,500 years. Over the centuries, Jews have been unyielding in their passionate commitment to Bible study on a daily basis. Then, at some point, they began applying that same passion to the understanding of scientific principles. Results of their scrupulous discipline are now evident in our everyday lives. Christians have done similarly, of course, but because they are two millennia behind the Jews, they will have to work a little harder to catch up.

by Michael Bash

There is no doubt in my mind that they will. I don't have to tell you that Gregor Mendel, founding genius of genetics, was an Augustinian monk, or that Sir Isaac Newton had a religious upbringing, or that even Charles Darwin, who attended Christian College and was buried at Westminster Abbey was, in his earlier years, on track to become a pastor.

Monotheist Islam, as supported by the Koran, claims many lasting achievements in science, as well— particularly from the period of its Golden Age, which saw significant advancements in medicine and literature, in addition to the development of algebra and algorithms, and even the game of chess.

Although these are the same religions that can be blamed for inspiring hatred, violence, and even all-out war over the centuries, it is important to make a distinction between the practice of religion based on its original precepts, and the exploitation of the religion based on blind ambition. Just as it is not money, but the love of money, in which greed finds root, it is not religion, but the exploitation of it, that creates so much chaos.

You, Vic Stenger, along with Richard Dawkins and Christopher Hitchens, were all raised in Christian homes, had Christian-based educations, and were directly or indirectly influenced by the Bible. If you had been born in Bangkok instead of Bayonne, you would not likely be a scientist today or writing books that take such satisfaction in refuting religion. If Darwin had first seen the light of day in a remote African village instead of civilized Shropshire, England, we might never have tapped into his knowledge of natural selection or the Darwinian theory of evolution.

Fads fade over the years. Old trends give way to new ones. Even cultists lose their cravings for the latest craze in cults. And yet, believers in the Bible remain as steadfast in their faith-based belief system as you do in your demand for physical evidence. Since no sound-minded scientist believes that there is nothing in this universe left to discover, it would be wise, as we move forward as a civilization, to consider other avenues of opportunity — including the perilous path of faith. Is it possible that there is something here that you and your colleagues are not taking seriously simply because it cannot be explained by any of the five senses? A major tenet of our judicial system comes to mind: *Innocent until proven guilty.* What if we turned things around here? What if we asked the scientific community to prove unequivocally that there is no God, and demand nothing less than physical evidence on its part? I take comfort in the fact that even Dawkins hedged his bet when he asserted, "Why there *almost* certainly is no God." And you have hedged yours by your willingness to believe, once you are confronted with the evidence. Even professional atheist Bill Maher is willing to eat his witty pronouncements, should he ever be provided with that elusive thing called proof.

It appears to me that, to borrow a line from *Hamlet,* *"you [all] protest too much."* If millions of people believed in something that I thought was ridiculous, but it made them feel good, and it wasn't directly hurting anyone, I would wish them good luck with a wink, and move on.

I accept the fact that you do not believe. My question to you is, would you like to believe? I suspect, at the bottom of it all, you would, and here, in part, may be why.

The following was written by the late Dag Hammarskjold, a wise, rational, and accomplished member of the 20th century's enlightened global community. *"God does not die on the day when we cease to believe in a personal deity, but we die on the day when our lives cease to be illuminated by the steady radiance, renewed daily, of a wonder, the source of which is beyond all reason."*

Shalom,

Michael

CHAPTER FOURTEEN
PEACE BETWEEN SCIENCE & RELIGION

Can There Be Permanent Peace?

When reading the Bible or the Talmud, it becomes evident that elements of fact and fiction are indiscriminately interwoven. Apparently in ancient times it was common to intermingle the two written forms and then leave it to the reader to differentiate one from the other. The Talmud makes a point of distinguishing between its unique categories of content: the Hallachah (the law) and the Agadah (the legend). It delves into deep discussions from a legal perspective, and provides stress relief with legends of the sages.

The Bible contains several classic allegories, which, although their purpose is instructional, should not be taken literally. A few such examples are: 1) the spineless, yet upright, serpent speaking in human language to Eve in the Garden of Eden, 2) the building of the Tower of Babel and subsequent consequences, and 3) Joshua commanding the sun to remain fixed in the sky for an extra day, allowing him to bring a war to an end.

That generation for whom the Bible was written was not sufficiently knowledgeable of the world to allow for a keen understanding of actual events. Even now, these three millennia later, and having come a long way, we are not yet fully there. So instead of reading incomprehensible accounts of what really took place, these primitive people were served up a series of stories that provided them with the intended message, but in a formula they were capable of digesting.

Over the millennia, it has been the choice of several groups within all three Abrahamic religions to adhere to their belief in the literal truth of the Bible, regardless

of mounting evidence to the contrary. The reason is simple. Their faith provides them with a comfort zone that answers every one of their questions to their profound satisfaction.

Yet, as scientists dig deeper for answers to the most stubborn of eternal questions, those arguing on behalf of

the literal truth face escalating scrutiny and skepticism. Eventually, science will have put forth so much conflicting evidence that true believers will no longer be able to cite evolutionary "gaps" to discount scientific theory. At that point, they will have no alternative but to modify their perspective or find new justification for their illogical perspective.

It can never be stressed often enough that the Bible was not written to be understood literally, and was accompanied by an essential companion guide, the Oral Law—the Talmud. Yet, when Christianity was founded 1,000 years later, the essential guide was completed disregarded, and remains so to this day. One has to wonder why.

Today, Christianity has everything to gain by accepting the Oral Bible. Doing so would almost automatically set the stage for a lasting peace and productive alliance between science and religion. However, such a harmonious union will never come easily, even in the minds of reasonable, intelligent, and logical thinkers. It is difficult if not impossible, after all, to alter or dispel a belief system instilled in us from early childhood that gains approval from our community and peer group. There is an alternative solution worth considering, for now. Should the leadership of various Christian and Orthodox Jewish groups become inspired to acknowledge the facts, they would automatically be modifying their belief systems, not by renouncing them, but by adding to them.

The following credo, or a variation thereof, might serve as a first step in that direction: "I believe in the literal truth of the Bible and the basic truth of its allegories."

The Internet is replete with round-the-clock heated debates that stoke the ongoing controversy between science and religion. Multitudes of individuals and organizations spend millions of dollars annually to defend, explain, or embellish the Bible.

Distinguished authors in both camps—creationists and atheists—have the provocative subject matter directly to thank for their celebrity and millions of annual book sales.

All of this expenditure of effort and money by those on either side of the issue would no longer be necessary the moment that true believers adopt the credo I stipulated three short paragraphs earlier: "I believe in the literal truth of the Bible and the basic truth of its allegories."

From the day this level of rationale is adopted by traditional religiosity, permanent peace between religion and science will be established, as well as a future in which they can work together to create a more functioning and flourishing world population. *

CHAPTER FIFTEEN
GOD GOOGLES GRAVITY

*An Argument in Favor of God as
Creator of the Universe*

The recent bestseller, *The Grand Design*, is the latest attempt by scientist Stephen Hawking and his co-author Leonard Mlodinow to answer the age-old questions: When and how did the universe begin? Why are we here? Why is there something rather than nothing? What is the nature of reality? Why are the laws of nature so finely tuned to accommodate the existence of humans? Does the universe need a Creator?

For many centuries, people believed that the universe had always existed. Once the Big Bang theory was postulated, it set the stage for an argument in favor of God as Creator of the universe.

In 1915, Albert Einstein formulated his theory, E=MC2. Still under the assumption that the universe was static, he factored into his theory an antigravity force that he believed blocked the universe from imploding. The force, to which Einstein added a cosmological constant, did not come from a particular source, but was built into the fabric of space-time.

When the Big Bang theory was discovered, Einstein eliminated the constant from his formula, which he called "the biggest blunder of my life." Surprisingly, in 1998, his cosmological constant was resurrected when it was discovered that the universe was expanding at such an accelerated rate that it needed a repulsive force to justify it. The constant is the "fine-tuner" element in the theory that points to the God who made the universe in the specific manner he did in order to enable life as we know it to survive, thrive, and perpetuate.

In *The Grand Design*, the authors come up with the following answer to the universe's remarkable fine-tuning phenomenon, categorically denying God as the fine-tuner. They explain: "That is not the answer of modern science...

"Our universe seems to be one of many, each with different laws. That multiverse idea... is a consequence of the no-boundary condition, as well as many other theories of modern cosmology. But if it's true, then the strong anthropic principle can be considered effectively equivalent to the weak one, putting the fine-tunings of physical law on the same footing as the environmental factors, for it means that our cosmic habitat—now the entire observable universe—is only one of many, just as our solar system is one of many. That means that in the same way that the environmental coincidences of our solar system were rendered unremarkable by the realization that billions of such systems exist, the fine-tunings in the laws of nature can be explained by the existence of multiple universes...

"The multiverse concept can explain the fine-tuning of physical law without the need for a benevolent creator who made the universe for our benefit."

In the last chapter of the book, the authors write: "Why is there something rather than nothing? Why do we exist? Why this particular set of laws and not some other?

"Some would claim the answer to these questions is that there is a God who chose to create the universe that way. It is reasonable to ask who or what created the universe, but if the answer is God, then the question has merely been deflected to that of who created God...We claim, however, that it is possible to answer these questions purely within the realm of science and without invoking any divine beings."

The authors go on to explain how the law of gravity is essential to the existence of the universe and the reason that

it can be created from nothing: "Because gravity shapes space and time, it allows space-time to be locally stable but globally unstable.

"On the scale of the entire universe, the positive energy of the matter *can* be balanced by the negative gravitational energy, and so there is no restriction on the creation of whole universes. Because there is a law like gravity, the universe can and will create itself from nothing...Spontaneous creation is the reason there is something rather than nothing, why the universe exists, why we exist. It is not necessary to invoke God to light the blue touch paper and set the universe going."

This conclusion on the part of the authors is wrong, for two reasons. First, they define God as a creator when he was actually a lawgiver, who gave natural laws to the universe and moral laws to humankind. Why should celestial bodies pull each other toward themselves? Why does the earth pull at us? At this moment in time, one can only conclude that this is God's secret. Second, the authors claim that the universe can be created from nothing. They are wrong here, as well. It may seem as though it is nothing because matter and anti-matter cancel each other out. But if the balance is disturbed slightly, an entire universe appears spontaneously.

Isaac Newton defined gravity as a force, one that attracts any one object to any other object. Albert Einstein defined gravity as the result of curvature of space-time. These are the most common theories used to explain the law of gravity. When Newton publicized his theory of gravity in the 1680s, it sparked the idea that gravity is a predictable force that acts on all matters in the universe, and is a function of mass and distance. Albert Einstein contributed his alternate theory in the early 1900s that did not perceive gravity as a force, but as a distortion in the shape of space-time, also commonly known as the fourth dimension. More recent scientists conjecture in terms of a graviton, which, according to *Weisstein's World of Physics*, "is a theoretical particle having no mass and no charge that carries the gravitational force" and essentially cause objects to be attracted to one another.

Basically, gravity is a mystery, and no one knows with certainty precisely how it works. We do recognize that the existence of gravity causes us to speculate about its essence and its similarity to other laws of attraction, such as found in love, friendship, and the multiple forms of affinity.

Ultimately, there is a difference between traditional nothing and God's version of nothing. To explain: Let's assume a friend owns apartment buildings worth $200 million. The value of the mortgage on the buildings is $100 million. Because of the present economy, the value of the buildings is now reduced to 50% of its original worth. That leaves our friend's current net worth at zero, even though he owns all those valuable assets. One day the market will recover and his $100 million net worth will be restored to him. In this manner of relativity, some "nothings" carry within them the nucleus of "everything." ✐

CHAPTER SIXTEEN
THE TWO BIBLES

*The Written Bible Was Never Intended
for Literal Interpretation*

During the Bronze Age, about 1,000 years before the birth of Christianity, the Bible was given to Moses and the Israelites after they departed Egypt in search of the Promised Land. In order to present the text to an entire nation of people, God (or whoever it was who actually wrote the Bible) was forced to confront a dilemma: how to tell the true story of Creation to a mass of people who were not yet sufficiently developed to grasp such complex theories as the Big Bang and evolution. God's quandary was similar to the one about the parents confronted by their child with the eternal question, "Where did I come from?" Using the same tactic as the average parent, God told a story that was based on a simple variation of the truth. His purpose was to make it comprehensible and palatable to the

mindset of that generation—and simultaneously allow the reader to feel good about himself.

Thus, the story of Adam and Eve was born. Of course, the truth is far different from the story in Genesis, since it has long been established that humans evolved over time from one-cell organisms that originated within the earth, then later divided into two cells, and so on. By using the Adam and Eve story, God was able to describe the beginning of the evolutionary process that started with earth and then skip to the end result, which was man. In the interests of simplicity, He merely disregarded the lengthy and complex midsection process of evolution.

Because religious belief is a powerful emotion instilled in us from childhood, it is naturally inflexible and difficult to change. As our knowledge of this world increases, and we no longer feel the profound need to believe in the God of our Fathers—the one depicted by our less knowledgeable ancestors—we can hope to modify our perspectives accordingly.

God and Moses knew all this, and when the Written Bible was given to the Israelites, and subsequently to the Jewish people, it was accompanied, as we know, by the Oral Bible. The Written Bible was never intended for literal interpretation. It was to be used with the aid of the Oral Bible, allowing it to evolve from generation to generation, and to adapt to the sensibilities of the time. Eventually, the Oral Bible was transcribed into the six books of the Talmud, which subsequently permitted newer interpretations through greater understanding, such as those to be found in the Shulchan Aruch.

The Talmud was not written until some time between the 1st century AD and the 5th, and the first Christians had apparently not been made aware of the Oral Bible. Therefore, it was not incorporated into their religion. But the Oral Bible had been an integral part of the Written Bible for 1,000 years before Christianity, remaining crucial to religious study

to this day, because it provides that all-essential feature—
permission to evolve.

Bible stories are either read as fact or are used more practically as teaching tools. The story of the Tower of Babel teaches that when people are united in common cause, there is nothing they can't accomplish. When we read the story relating the source of Original Sin, we should be fully aware that while it is based on the truth, it was written in a way that could be understood by the primitive readers of that period.

In the final analysis, everything evolves, including the significance of words. Were this not the case, dictionaries would never have need to modify or expand their content—and it is common knowledge that they do so on an annual basis. ❦

CHAPTER SEVENTEEN
THE LITERAL TRUTH OF
THE BIBLE

A Simple Safeguard, A Major Obstacle

Belief in the literal truth of the Bible is a simple but ironclad strategy for defending Biblical text in its entirety. Based on this principle, charging just one statement of the Bible to be false, however inconsequential, questions the authenticity of every other statement throughout the text. "God wrote the Bible. God is omniscience. God is faultless." Based on this traditional belief system, the Bible is literally perfect.

While this precept sounds good in theory, there are three valid reasons not to practice this belief.

1) As God states to Moses in Exodus 3:14: *"I will be that which I will be,"* He wants us to know that He evolves, and, since He evolves, so does everything else, including humankind and the Bible. An "evolving" Bible cannot also be termed "literal." However, if one insists on believing in the literal truth, then one must also believe in the literal truth of Exodus: 3:14, which, as we know, opens the door to evolution.

2) The Bible was not presented directly to Christianity. It was given to Moses 3,300 years ago on Mount Sinai, 1,000 years prior to the birth of Christ, who gave it to the elders of Israel, and on down the line. Over time, changes and updates were made through the Oral Law, which came to

be known as the Talmud, but, as we know, the Christian church did not adopt those changes, as they were either not aware of the Oral Law or simply preferred to adhere to the "Word of God" in the original text. One of these laws pertained to charging interest for a business loan.

3) Science and Technology are the best tools we have to advance civilization. Believing in the literal truth of the Bible presents a major obstacle to scientific progress.

The literal truth holds us fixed in the world of 3,300 years ago, while, in reality, we live in a vastly different 21st century. Life has evolved significantly since the Bible was written. Contemporary society does not relate to the literal truth of the Adam and Eve story in which a serpent tempts Eve to eat the fruit of the tree of "Knowledge of Good and Evil." ✎

BIBLICAL STORIES WERE NEVER MEANT TO BE UNDERSTOOD AS FACT.

✎ Biblical Stories were intended to be acceptable to the sensibilities of that ancient generation for which they were written. While on many levels, The Bible is out of step with modern society, it also has an almost infinite number of positive attributes to which we can still relate, and is the  reason it remains the best-selling book of all time. The most significant of these is its enormous influence on Western Civilization, which includes the fields of science, technology and medicine. It is apparent that Western Civilization has far outpaced the accomplishments of Eastern Civilization, and this is due in large part to the influences of the Bible on our culture.

Should modern Christian leaders finally see the logic and the enormous advantage in adapting the Oral Law

to the original principles of the Written Bible, it is bound
to resolve any further conflicts between science and
religion, and remove age-old impediments to scientific
and technological advancements. By contrast, by insisting
on the literal truth, those believers, perhaps unwittingly,
discourage future generations from the pursuit of certain
careers and lifestyles, which compromise our full potential
in the eternal pursuit of knowledge.

The saddest example of how belief in the literal truth
can affect a person's life is illustrated on pages 321- 322
of Richard Dawkins's book, *The God Delusion*. He states:
"The American geologist Kurt Wise was a highly qualified
and genuinely promising young scientist, well on his way
to achieving his dream of teaching science and doing
research at a proper university. Then tragedy struck. It
came not from outside, but from within his own mind, a
mind fatally subverted and weakened by a fundamentalist
religious upbringing that required him to believe that the
earth—the subject of his Chicago and Harvard geological
education was less than ten thousand years old. He was
too intelligent not to recognize the head-on collision
between his religion and his science, and the conflict in his
mind made him increasingly uneasy. One day, he could
bear the strain no more and he clinched the matter with
a pair of scissors. He took a Bible and went right through
it, literally cutting out every verse that would have to go
if the scientific worldview were true. At the end of this
ruthlessly honest and labour-intensive exercise, there
was so little left of his Bible that, 'try as I might, and even
with the benefit of intact margins throughout the pages
of Scripture, I found it impossible to pick up the Bible
without it being rent in two. I had to make a decision
between evolution and Scripture. Either the Scripture was
true and evolution was wrong or evolution was true and
I must toss out the Bible... It was there that night that I
accepted the Word of God and rejected all that would ever

counter it, including evolution. With that, in great sorrow, I tossed into the fire all my dreams and hopes in science.'"

What a senseless tragedy! Imagine, instead, a world that is not locked into believing in the literal truth of the Bible: a world without guilt, and yet one that in no way corrupts the original integrity of the Bible. Americans cherish freedom more than anything. With this new freedom from guilt to study and pursue advancements in all fields of science and technology, America would forge ahead as never before, well ahead of all other nations—well ahead, even, of our own previous generations.

Ultimately, when science discovers the most elusive answer of all the mysteries of the universe—the theory of everything—it will fulfill God's long-held goal for man: "We will be that which will be," thereby creating a life on earth that is longer, healthier, and forever at harmony and peace with one another.

PEACEFUL COEXISTENCE BETWEEN RELIGION AND SCIENCE

The Oral Law (Oral Torah) is the perpetual steppingstone to a peaceful coexistence between religion and science. It is the set of instructions for proper use and understanding of the Old Testament. Because Christianity has overlooked this handy compendium for 2,000 years, it is no wonder that some denominations of the faith have long depended solely on Biblical content for their absolute truth.

Bible Professor Emeritus Uriel Simon of Bar-Ilan University's Zalman Shamir Bible Department says that his department "has always contended with the tension between commitment to faith and tradition and accepting the proven results of scientific research.

"...One of the main aspects of religious fundamentalism," he says, "is the belief that Scripture has a fixed eternal authorized meaning, and we are bound by it. According to this approach, if the Torah says 'an eye for an eye' it means

gouging out the eye of the assailant, just as the hands of thieves are still cut off in Saudi Arabia. In contrast, we should believe in the main principle of the Oral Law, according to which the Torah renews itself constantly through the authentic interpretation of teachers of the Law. Just as the Rabbis intended 'an eye for an eye' to mean monetary compensation, we must also ask ourselves responsibly and honestly about any issue—national, political, moral, legal, social (e.g., the status of women)—what is the true interpretation of the verses of the Torah in contemporary conditions?"

Is it permissible to re-interpret Scripture? Professor Simon says: "It depends on the balance between real commitment to the holiness and the truth of Torah, and the recognition of the need to find interpretations that match the pressing needs of the hour. The Ultra-Orthodox argument against Religious Zionism is well known, that in principle it is like Reform Judaism, since ostensibly there is no clear limit to innovation. In truth, all authentically religious people know that there are borders, which are determined by our sincere understanding, responsibility and devotion. A living religion succeeds in combining continuity and change."

In response to the question of Biblical criticism and modern scientific discoveries, Professor Simon says: "the correct answer here is dialectical. In any instance of conflict between religious belief and scientific conclusion, we must get to the root of the collision and precisely delimit its realm. When there is no choice, you can offer a new interpretation of religious faith in the way laid out by Maimonides in The Guide for the Perplexed (2:25)."

Regarding inconsistencies between archaeological finds and Biblical text, the professor said: "the archaeologist must distinguish facts from interpretation. Secular archaeologists can reach far-fetched conclusions from the lack of findings, such as the absence of any material or textual evidence of the bondage of Israelis in Egypt and the miracle of the Exodus. I admit that this is indeed a disturbing reality, that ancient Egyptian literature remembers neither Joseph nor Moses, nor the near-cosmic event of the Ten Plagues."

He suggests a solution that would "turn the text into a metaphor, which is clearly a homiletic tool. This is the way that Ahad Ha'am chose in his article, "Moses," in which he claimed that it doesn't matter whether Moses was a historical figure or a literary figure; the important thing is the heritage embodied in his personality. However, this technique should not be used too often, because the factual truth has a unique persuasive power compared to artistic truth. [It is best to] adhere to the maximal historicity of the Bible as long as it is not contradicted by proven facts, while maintaining rigorous intellectual honesty. Only when this historicity is undermined, we have the 'safety net' of legitimate metaphorizing."

Professor Simon's voice is one of reason and intellect, and should reverberate soundly throughout our contemporary culture worldwide. ❧

CHAPTER EIGHTEEN
BAR-ILAN UNIVERSITY

Quintessential Model for Peaceful
Coexistence Between Religion and Science

An excellent example of the fruitful coexistence between science and religion is found at Bar-Ilan University, Israel's largest institute of higher learning, with a student body of nearly 35,000 from diverse cultural and religious backgrounds who study and work together harmoniously in their classrooms, laboratories, and libraries. Besides its distinguished community of hundreds of scientists engaged in cutting edge research and development, the university also boasts a group of archeological scholars who research physical evidence of Biblical characters. Their first discovery was of Goliath.

Bar-Ilan University's unique community of scientists conduct themselves in accordance with the Jewish tradition, investing their energy and efforts into the integration of the old with the new, the ancient with the modern, the sacred with the mundane, the spiritual with the scientific.

It is interesting to note that the Bar-Ilan University logo

is a fusing together of the first two letters of the Hebrew alphabet: Aleph and Bet, and reflects the dual aims of the University: the pursuit of academic excellence and the study of Jewish heritage. Aleph signifies the search for divine wisdom and Bet alludes to creation and the scientific realm.

According to the university's website, it "regards the sacred principles of Judaism as the manifestation of the Jewish people's uniqueness, in accordance with the principles defined upon its establishment. The university's basic roles include the safeguarding of these principles out of love and with the purpose of training and producing scholars, researchers, and men of science knowledgeable in the Torah and imbued with the original Jewish spirit and love of one's brethren."

What makes Bar-Ilan University unique in recent years is that it has expanded its research activities and advanced studies by substantially increasing the number of research students via presidential and other scholarships. The university has also developed unique interdisciplinary study programs, and has intensified research and instruction in fields that are at the forefront of sciences, such as: computational biology, biotechnology, nanotechnology and more.

From its globally recognized leadership in nanotechnology, Biblical archeology, and engineering to its 1,800 Judaism-related courses offered under the auspices of the world's largest Jewish studies faculty, Bar-Ilan University is making its impact felt as it meshes the microscope and Torah scroll.

I recently met the president of Bar Ilan University, Professor Moshe Kaveh. After talking with him, I understood why Bar Ilan is so successful. He should be lecturing in every church and synagogue, convincing people that religion and science can work together in harmony. 𝄢

CHAPTER NINETEEN
IS RELIGION GOOD
FOR YOU?

*Which is of Greater Value: Going to the Church
or the Gym?*

*"If something is in me which can be called religious, then it is
the unbounded admiration for the structure of the world so far
as our science can reveal it."*

– Albert Einstein

In the June 4, 2000 edition of the London Sunday
Times, Dr. Raj Pasuud wrote: "Want to live longer? Medical
research from the National Institute of Healthcare Research
in America suggests you might be better attending church
than going to the gym."

This study shows that religious people have lower
blood pressure than the nonreligious. "The odds of
survival for people who rated higher on measures of
public and private religious involvement were 29% higher
than those people who scored lower on such measures."

The article continues: "Science also finds support for

Go to The Gym?

For while bodily training is of
some value, godliness is of value
in every way, as it holds promise
for the present life and also for
the life to come.   Timothy 4:8

the idea that religious involvement is
helpful beyond the more mundane
benefits of group support. For example,
recent research on Israeli Kibbutzim,
which are usually cohesive supportive
communities, established that living
in more religious kibbutzim was
associated with considerably lower
mortality than secular ones."

Why have almost all human

beings in every known culture believed in God (or gods), and accepted the customs, dogmas, and institutions created by different religions?

Why would such great scientists as: Augustine, Aquinas, Descartes, Newton, William James, and even Einstein become religious believers?

Research shows that religion is very good for those who practice it, as well as for society as a whole. Religious people are happier, more charitable, have more stable families, and contribute more to their communities.

What proves the benefits of religion the most are those nonreligious people who became religious. One study made by Professor Armand Nicholi, Jr. states: "Several years ago I conducted a research project exploring Harvard University students who, while undergraduates, experienced what they referred to as a 'religion conversion.' I interviewed those students, as well as people who knew them before and after their conversion. Were these experiences an expression of pathology, i.e., isolating and destructive, or were they adaptive and constructive? Did these experiences enhance or impair functioning? Results published in the *American Journal of Psychiatry* stated that each subject described a "marked improvement in ego functioning [including] a radical change in lifestyle with an abrupt halt in the use of drugs, alcohol, and cigarettes; improved impulse control with adoption of a strict sexual code demanding chastity or marriage with fidelity; improved academic performance; enhanced self-image and greater access to inner feelings; an increased capacity for establishing 'close, satisfying relationships'; improved communication with parents, though most parents at first expressed some degree of alarm over the student's rather sudden, intense religious interest; a positive change in affect, with a lessening of 'existential despair'; and a decrease in preoccupation with the passage of time and apprehension over death."

by Michael Bash

Another good description of the benefits of religion is given by Dr. Harold Koenig of Duke University. "The benefit of devout religious practice, particularly involvement in a faith community and religious commitment, [is] that people cope better. In general, they cope with stress better, they experience greater well being because they have more hope, they're more optimistic, they experience less depression, less anxiety, and they commit suicide less often. They don't drink alcohol as much, they don't use drugs as much, they don't smoke cigarettes as much, and they have healthier lifestyles. They have stronger immune systems, lower blood pressure, probably better cardiovascular functioning, and probably a healthier hormonal environment physiologically—particularly with respect to cortisol and adrenaline [stress hormones].

And they live longer."

Sociobiology, a new branch of human behavioral science, popularized by Edward O. Wilson of Harvard University, has done extensive study to find the biological reasons humans need religion.

To understand how religion develops, we can look at the development of language. No animal has anything like our language capacity. That is because only the human brain has two specialized zones: Broca's Area and Wermicke's Area (both on the left side), in which the neurons are so connected they form a mechanism that recognizes the relationships among words in sentences. The brain is constructed in such a way that even children can generally figure out what people around them are communicating.

Religion works similarly. As Professor Walter Burkert

105

of the University of Zurich says: "We may view religion parallel to language...a long-lived hybrid between cultural and biological traditions." He believes that we have biological capacities that cause us to need, learn, value, and practice religion.

Sociobiologists have always maintained that mankind has needs that are met by religion. It is a way for people to allay their fears of the world's mystifying phenomena that they can explain in no other way. With the development of the brain's capacity for language, humans have been able to develop concepts that were unavailable to pre-humans, including: the awareness of risk and death, of time, of both the past and the future, reward and punishment, satisfaction of problem solving and aesthetic pleasures, and wonder and awe.

Most humans, from the ancient times to today, make sense of all their mystifying negative and positive experiences by means of religion. Against the uncertainties and dangers of the future, people pray, asking God for a positive outcome. Against the tragedy of losing a loved one and the fear of death, humans seek reassurances that they will live after death in another world. Against injustice, inequality, and the unfairness of life's struggles, what is more reassuring than God's promise of just rewards in heaven? And when things are good, what is more appropriate than to thank God for all His loving support and generosity?

Religion also acts as a binding social force. Wilson says: "Religion is empowered mightily by its principle ally, tribalism. The shamans and priests implore us in somber cadence: "Trust in the sacred rituals. Become part of the immortal force[;] you are one of us."

While the benefits of church attendance are obvious, there is no reason to deny yourself the insurance of a gym membership, as well. ❧

CHAPTER TWENTY
A TOUCH OF SCIENCE IN THE BIBLE

*An Amazing Story In Genesis 30:27 Provides
Keen Insight into the Bible's View of Science*

In the story of Jacob, Laban (the father of his two wives, Rachel and Leah) asks him to stay on to "feed and keep" his flocks. When Jacob agrees to the task, Laban asks him what he wants as compensation. Jacob answers: *"Let me pass through all your flock today, removing from them all the speckled and spotted sheep, and all the brown ones among the lambs, and the spotted and speckled among the goats, and these shall be my wages."* (Genesis 30:32) Because brown lambs and spotted and speckled sheep and goats were well in the minority, Laban agreed to what seemed like a deal biased in his favor.

Over time, Jacob found a method for producing many more brown lambs and speckled and spotted sheep and goats from his herds than are generally found in nature. He applied his knowledge and created a breeding system that would result in a large number of these animals. *"Thus the man became exceedingly prosperous and had large flocks, female and male servants, and camels and donkeys."* (Genesis 30:43)

Here the Bible clearly describes how research can produce a valuable tool that, effectively applied, is capable of creating vast wealth for its entrepreneurial inventor. Science is great! How do we know? The Bible tells us so. ℓ

CHAPTER TWENTY-ONE
THE CHOSEN PLANET

An Interesting Parallel Between
Planet Earth and the Jewish People

According to the Bible, God chose Abraham and his descendants to communicate their monotheistic belief to the entire world. This conviction of our one God began with the small nation of Israelites—the ancient Jews—and remained with them for 1,000 years before spreading like wildfire to the rest of the world through Christianity and Islam.

Recent discoveries provide convincing evidence that we here on earth are probably alone in the universe. For more than 20 years, the SETI Institute has been searching for intelligent life elsewhere in space, using technology capable of telegraphing their existence. The likelihood that there exists on one of the incalculable trillions of stars in the universe a species comparable to humankind and in possession of advanced communications capabilities is remote, at best, but based on the efforts being made, it was hoped that SETI would receive at least one intelligent signal suggesting the existence of extraterrestrial life. So far, however, there has been nothing but silence

From our primitive perspective of the past, the earth was the center of the universe, and we were created directly by God. That concept made us feel special and unique as a species. Since then, we have discovered that the universe is vast and that earth is only one simple component of a small solar system tucked into a remote part of our galaxy—the Milky Way—which contains billions of other planets, many larger than ours.

by Michael Bash

The more we know about the enormous universe in which we live, the more insignificant we seem, by comparison. We began as giants, at least, in terms of our limited knowledge, and over the eons we have been reduced to the level of ants or less. Some of us might ask, *why would God even bother with us and why would we be deserving of a personal God?* As religious as Einstein was by his own admission, he also declared his skepticism of the existence of a personal God.

The probability that we are alone in this infinite universe should provide us with sufficient evidence to believe we are more important than we might previously have thought. Rather than ants or even giants, we are of greater stature still, by immeasurable degrees. Some scientists believe that one day we will be able to travel to other solar systems and galaxies for the purpose, not only of visiting, but for populating deep space with humankind.

The latest event in space exploration took place on August 5, 2012 with the flawless touchdown on the surface of Mars by NASA's $2.5 billion Curiosity rover. Its plans were to spend the next 2-1/2 years studying the Gale Crater for signs that the Red Planet might ever have supported microbial life.

Similar to the way God originally designated a tiny nation on a small planet in a remote solar system to spread His word, He may, one day, depend on us to spread His message into infinity—and beyond.

As a human being, how does that make you feel? The logical answer is, Chosen!

CHAPTER TWENTY-TWO
MODERN SCIENTIFIC DISCOVERIES

Documented 2,000-3,300 Years Ago in the Written and Oral Torah

It has long been established by religious scholars that the Bible and related ancient texts contain numerous examples of scientific knowledge that are generally attributed to the works of modern research.

The following few samples make a powerful argument for Biblical knowledge that reached far beyond the scope of our primitive ancestors:

THE BIG BANG THEORY IS CONFIRMED IN GENESIS.

The Bible tells us: *In the beginning, God created the Heaven and the Earth.* [Genesis 1:1] Prior to the "Big Bang" theory, scientists believed that the universe had always existed, that there was no "beginning."

THE EARTH IS SHAPED LIKE A BALL, SUSPENDED IN SPACE.

In the Zohar (Book of Splendor), which was written 2,000 years ago, it states: *The world and the people who inhabit it are turning around like a ball. Half of them are on the upper part of the ball and the other half are on the bottom of the ball. And the people that live on the two different parts of this ball look different from one another, with different-looking faces, because the climate varies from place to place. When there is light to half of them, there is night to the other half. And there is a place in the world where the day is very, very long, and the night is very short. And this secret was given to all the sages of the Torah.*

FROM ONE CONTINENT CAME SEVERAL.

It is apparent from looking at the map that all the continents originally fitted together. For example, the east coast configuration of South America fits into the west coast configuration of Africa. The Torah, written 3,300 years ago, refers to the existence of one block of land by stating: *And God said: "the water under the sky should go in one place, the land in another place. One piece. One here and one there."*

One thousand years later, the Zohar talks about the split. But in the Bible, it states: *God is the one that moves mountains, and moves the earth from one place to the other, and they all split apart.* (Job 9:5) This is mentioned in the Talmud, as well.

THE BIBLE VERIFIES THAT AIR HAS WEIGHT.

Thousands of years ago, it was believed that air was weightless. We have learned since then that is an erroneous statement, and that weight is required, among other things, for planes to fly in mid-air. Evagelista Torricelli discovered this in 1640.

LIGHTNING WAS HARNESSED WELL BEFORE BENJAMIN FRANKLIN FLEW HIS KITE.

It is widely believed that Benjamin Franklin discovered the lightning rod in the 18th century. The Talmud, written 2,000 years earlier, states that: ...*a person should not put a metal rod among chickens, because this is how the Elamites do it, and it is not our way.* However, the Talmud allows an individual to use a metal rod to catch the lightning. (Tractate Shabbat, Chapter 7) Centuries later, Benjamin Franklin is reputed to have used a kite during a rainstorm, and gotten the same results.

ENERGY AND MATTER ARE ETERNAL.

Matter could be converted into energy and back again. So it is stated in the Bible, Ecclesiastes, which is attributed to the 2,800 years old writings of King Solomon: *I knew that everything that God does will remain forever...You cannot add to it and you cannot deduct from it. It preserves itself.* The Talmud states: *It is not possible for an earthly body to disappear. Even if you set him on fire, he does not disappear from the world.* What this confirms in 21st century terms is that energy never dies, pure and simple. This is Einstein's theory of $E=MC2$, which he discovered in the 20th century.

Another section of the Bible refers to the red heifer that was used for sacrifice and for the removal of a particular sin. The Bible states that the red heifer must be checked in eighteen places to determine the state of its health. Moses advised that, contrary to popular belief, she did not have to be cut up in order to determine her health. Rather, a pillar of smoke positioned in front of her would give

112

visual access to her organs. And based on his advice, that is what was done.

SOUND (OR VOCAL) WAVES INFLUENCE MATTER.

A chemistry student gave a speech at the University of Bar Ilan in Israel. He said: "I took three plates, and in each one I put beans atop a layer of cotton. For two weeks I daily applied water from the faucet to the first one, but did nothing else. The second one, I gave water from the faucet, and cursed it repeatedly for the full two weeks. With the third one, I also used water from the faucet, but I read to it from the Book of Psalms and thanked God for our water and the food that he gives us. Within two weeks, I saw the difference. The one I did nothing for but water grew at an average rate. The one to which I read from Psalms and gave prayers to God grew twice as well. And the one that I cursed didn't grow at all." The Talmud states: *A person's talk and thoughts give power to upper places and influences what happens in this world.*

GENERAL ANESTHESIA WAS USED 2,000 YEARS AGO FOR SURGERY.

The Talmud tells the 2,000 year-old story of Rabbi Eliazer (son of Simon Bar Yohai) whose son was taken ill. After he was given a sleeping potion and put to bed, the boy's belly was torn open and "baskets of fat" were extracted. Thereafter, he was put back together, and was healed. (Tractate Baba Metseia 83:2)

AN EMBRYO BECOMES A FETUS AFTER THE 40TH DAY.

The Talmud says that: *If a woman has a miscarriage before the 40th day, she did not miscarry a baby.* The embryo becomes a fetus on the 41st day, when the brain begins to function, and not before, according to Talmudic law. Twenty-first century technology gives evidence that the embryo becomes a fetus at the end of the eighth week of pregnancy, or approximately on the 56th day. Considering the advances in technology that it took to make that latter determination, it must be concluded that the two figures are not so far apart.

TWINS ARE CONCEIVED SIMULTANEOUSLY.

In ancient times, it was believed that in order for a woman to conceive twins, she would have to have sex with her husband on two separate occasions. A story in the Talmud relates of a man who slept with his wife once, and she became pregnant. Then he went away for three months. When his wife delivered, she had twins. The man was distraught over what he believed to be his wife's infidelity. He went to the sages, and told them that his wife must have slept with another man while he was away because she had twins, and he had only slept with her once during that period of her conception. The sages told him that he was wrong not to trust his wife, and that one embryo is capable of splitting in two. They told him: "We were advised by our teachers that a woman cannot conceive twice during one pregnancy. She conceives once, and that's it for the duration." The rabbi assured the man that there was one "drop," and that it simply divided into two. (Tractate Nidah, 27:1)

by Michael Bash

CIRCUMCISION IS PERFORMED ON THE EIGHTH DAY FOR REASONS OF HEALTH.

The Bible states that the reason not to perform circumcision before the eighth day is that the blood does not coagulate effectively until then, and therefore presents a greater risk the infant will bleed to death as a result of the procedure.

"Science can be created only by those who are thoroughly imbued with the aspiration toward truth and understanding. This source of feeling, however, springs from the sphere of religion.

"Science without religion is lame, religion without science is blind." ❦

- Albert Einstein

CHAPTER TWENTY-THREE
FREE WILL
WE HAVE IT, CONDITIONALLY.

According to The Grand Design, by Stephen Hawking and Leonard Mlodinow, we do not have free will. "Though we feel we can choose what we do, our understanding of the molecular basis of biology shows that biological processes are governed by the law of physics and chemistry and therefore are as determined as the orbits of the planets. Recent experiments in neuroscience support the view that it is our physical brain, following the known laws of science, that determine our actions, and not some agency that exists outside those laws. For example, a study of patients undergoing awake brain surgery found that by electrically stimulating the appropriate regions of the brain, one could create in the patient the desire to move the hand, arm, or foot, or to move the lips and talk. It is hard to imagine how free will can operate if our behavior is determined by physical law, so it seems that we are no more than biological machines and that free will is just an illusion.".

To reinforce their argument, the authors say: "Economics is also an effective theory, based on the notion of free will plus the assumption that people evaluate their possible alternative courses of action and choose the best. That effective theory is only moderately successful in predicting behavior because, as well we all know, decisions are often not rational or are based on analysis of the consequences of the choice. That is why the world is in such a mess."

Our current understanding is that the existence of free will is still an uncertainty, as it appears to be dependent on biology, and the fact that the body's reaction, the result of chemistry and physics, is predetermined: a classic example of cause and effect.

Two thousand years ago, the sages of the Talmud and their leader, Rabbi Akivah, concluded that there is limited free will: Hakol tsafooy ve' hareshoot netoonah or: All is foreseeable, and permission is granted. (Talmud; Tractate, Ethics of the Father) This would mean that, while everything is predictable, we do have permission to disturb that law, authorization for which comes from God. In other words it would seem that God permits us to make some decisions on our own; a particularly astute observation by the sages, considering it was made two millennia ago, before science made it possible for us to study this complicated issue under controlled conditions.

Modern science tells us that there are two factors controlling our behavior: our genes and our environment. So, people with different genes will react differently to the same conditions. From studies performed on twins, we find that, even those having grown up in different households, demonstrate more similar reactions to their environment than those who are biologically dissimilar.

This argument for limited free will provides incentive for proactivity. Rather than be passive about personal or environmental characteristics that are less than agreeable to us, we are required to exert additional effort to produce a desired change. That is why engaging in proactivity is so vital to a satisfying existence. Passive individuals, by nature, do not practice free will to the same extent as those who are naturally more aggressive. Ultimately, the permission is there to change the course of our lives, but unless we are willing to go outside of our comfort level, and experience some temporary measure of uneasiness in the process, we are likely to remain stuck in place. ❧

CHAPTER TWENTY-FOUR
BUILDING A BETTER WORLD

TIKKUN OLAM:
ANCIENT VISION REVISITED

Where there is no vision people will perish.
(Proverbs 29:18)

The most compelling and frequent argument against the existence of God is the issue of human suffering. We want to know why a benevolent God bears witness to all the abject misery in this world—natural disasters, disease, and starvation, as well as despicable acts of human violence—and yet does not use his power to stop it.

Pastor Burt D. Ehrman, a professor of religious studies at the University of North Carolina, Chapel Hill, wrote several books, the latest of which is, *God's Problem: How the Bible Fails to Answer Our Most Important Question—Why We Suffer.* Because Ehrman was unable to answer this pivotal question, he began losing his belief in the existence of God and eventually departed the church.

This eternal query about God stems from our conviction that He is supposed to be omnipotent, with full control of everything that happens in this universe, including the suffering of humankind. In accordance with this misunderstanding of God's alleged almighty power, we are only left to wonder why He permits such tragedy on His omniscient watch. Ah, but were we to have taken seriously God's earlier disclosure—in Exodus 3:14—that, rather than perfect, He was, and is, evolving, we would not expect Him to confer endless and unconditional joy on all His creatures.

With this greater understanding of God's limitations, we should now be better able to appreciate the vast marvels of the universe, including the defects built into the system, without which it would be unable to function as brilliantly as it does—if at all. In its glorious imperfection, therefore, the universe is as perfect as it is capable of being at this point in time—disasters and human failings notwithstanding.

So, while the bad news appears to be that God and His universe are, thus far, flawed, so are we as humans, for having been made in His image. That said, it would seem that we are also, therefore, destined to suffer all manner of natural and unnatural disasters well past the foreseeable future. What a dreadful state of affairs!

And yet, there is good news, as well. Precisely because God created us in His image, we are endowed with an extraordinary brain with which to reason. Our keen intelligence combined with our innate thirst for knowledge is, in fact, built into God's system to help us find myriad ways to solve our problems—all on our own.

On page 21 of his book, *Covenant & Conversation: Genesis*, Rabbi Jonathan Sacks states: "The fundamental point of Genesis 1 is that God transcends nature. Therefore, He is free, unbounded by nature's laws. By creating human beings 'in His image,' God gave us a similar freedom, thus creating the one being capable itself of being creative." The unprecedented account of God in the Torah's opening chapter leads to an equally unprecedented view of the human being and the capacity for self-transformation.

As early as the 2nd century, our fine intellect was already acknowledged. At that time, the Mishna portion of the Talmud coined the phrase *Tikkun Olam*—translated to mean "repairing the world"—and was used repeatedly thereafter, in the generations to follow. Kabbalist Rabbi Isaac Luria redefined the term in the 16th century, when it was expanded to mean "amending the world," with

by Michael Bash

emphasis on the "mystical idea of collecting broken sparks and establishing primordial harmony within the divine." Humans thus became God's partner in repairing what needed fixing on His earth. Now, in 21st century Israel, the term is appropriately applied to specific projects of a socially redeeming nature.

From my perspective, were all enlightened nations to join together and pool their resources for scientific and technological advances rather than to dissipate them on arms races and wars, humankind could accomplish the following goals, ultimately evolving this world closer to God's intended perfection than ever before:⌒

1. **Feed the World** - Objective: the total elimination of global starvation through the development of agricultural projects and systems designed to produce massive amounts of food as well as educational programs to teach underdeveloped nations how to create a sustainable food program for their population. While the United Nation's Food and Agricultural Organization (FAO) claims 925 million of the earth's population is currently under- or malnourished (mostly in Asia and the Pacific, followed by Sub-Sahara Africa, as well as Europe and North and South America), the FAO also states that there is sufficient worldwide food supply to keep all 6.8 billion of us from going to bed hungry at night. One has to wonder where the system breaks down to account for such staggering mismanagement.

Our first step would be to set up a private international nonprofit foundation to educate and enlighten representatives from other developed nations to join in the effort. As we define and refine our programs, we will be promoting them overseas in areas that are desperate for the training and for the crops from which their populations would benefit. Overall, agriculture is the most effective and quickest way to produce massive numbers of jobs. With a Feed the World program, we could train millions of workers to perform specialized functions in each phase of the operation. Primarily, we could recruit these individuals from the rolls of recent college graduates as well as the un- and underemployed and retirees. As a result, unemployment numbers would drop like a stone.

Just as the Jewish National Fund is dedicated to making the world a better place through agricultural innovation, renewable energy, and medical research, the Feed the World program would be funded primarily, not by mega-corporations, but by individual donations of pennies, dimes, and dollars. The program would essentially be inspired by a religious consciousness of tithing and reinforced with the intellectual know-how of 21st century science. In my Israeli schoolrooms, every teacher's desk had a charity box, into which it was a daily practice for children to drop their small change. After eight years of performing such a ritual, charity becomes a lifelong habit that passes down through the generations. Our project would expand on this ritual worldwide.

A couple of decades ago, I owned and operated a large ranch in Mineola, Texas, where I raised beef cattle. I also owned and operated two large dairy farms in Delano and Fresno, California, where I raised milk cows and, nearby, grew corn and alfalfa for their feed. I know how rewarding it is to do this kind of work—financially as well as emotionally. Feed the World could cultivate vast areas of the United States, reclaiming arid desert land for agriculture. With access to advanced technology, I believe we could achieve our goal in a relatively short period of time. Considering that America was known not long ago as "the breadbasket of the world," it would be natural for us to make a dramatic comeback in this manner—exporting 50% of our crops to other countries, which would pay for the program's costs, and donating the remaining 50% to needy nations, that, simultaneously, we would train to become agriculturally independent.

About 20 years ago, I read in *National Geographic* that the deserts of the world are continually expanding, with the notable exception of the land of Israel, based on the fact that it is continuously converting its arid land to fertile soil for agricultural use. This is the kind of result our plan would make possible through every participating country across the entire globe.

We would also consider advocating for a voluntary worldwide reduction of population growth, particularly in developing nations, as China has implemented in the past—a move that may be in large part responsible for its significant economic growth and stability over these past 10-20 years and its healthy projections into the future. By stabilizing world population, we could better maintain economic viability throughout. This would not be imposed by government mandate, but by education and birth control methods on an individual level.

2. **Heal the World** - Objective: The gradual elimination of all diseases through expanded scientific research, using state-of-the-art technology and surgical tools and techniques as well as the latest breakthroughs in stem cell research and genetic engineering.

Through continued exploration into the workings of the brain, science will likely one day be able to engineer hatred, fear, and intolerance from the human mind. What better way to ensure the end of conflict, warfare, hatred, and intolerance, which has always impeded human progress, holding us back from more admirable goals?

Furthermore, we could import researchers, scientists, and physicians from other countries to join our medical community with the common goal of discovering cures for the deadliest and most stubborn of human and animal diseases, as well as performing research into climate control and space exploration.

In the interim, the development of early-warning

devices and reinforcement of buildings would protect the world population from impending natural and man-made disasters. In addition, sections of the reclaimed deserts would be made habitable in order to move populations away from potentially dangerous areas to safer and more hospitable havens.

By setting up an international program with foreign students and experts in their respective fields, we would prepare them to return to their country of origin, where they would continue to work toward the program's objectives, ultimately promoting a healthy and harmonious planet and population.

3. **Free the World of Negativity** - Objective: The development of super-smart computer technology designed to make decisions consistently resulting in best outcome, and that are free of emotional bias or human error. Research and development of effective techniques could eliminate the impact of negative emotions on the same frontier as it could be conquered through medical research. (See #2 above: Heal the World.) Along with medical research and engineering of the human brain that could eliminate negative emotions from our DNA, we would be able to rid the human race and the earth of deadly conflict and disharmony.

As we tap into our vast underutilized human resources we create an international team of specialists and experts: introducing Team Tikkun Olam—its primary objective to repair and amend the world.

Ultimately, religion would continue to concentrate its focus on those traditional functions and rituals that include: prayer, ethnics, morality, family values, charity, etc., while scientists would exert their efforts and energies toward the research that will continue to produce breakthroughs in health, lifestyle, and a greater knowledge of the universe.

What better conclusion to reach than that while separately religion and science have been stunted by the differences between them, in harmony, they provide the engine to fast-track evolution as never before. It's not such a stretch, after all, when you consider that, separately, man and woman are restricted from fully exploiting their natural abilities, but together comprise the formula to ensure the infinite continuity of humankind.

God evolves. And so do we. But if we expect God to keep evolving for our benefit, it is our obligation to match His efforts with our own. Inspired by Tikkun Olam, and supported by Team Tikkun Olam, we move forward as never before.

"Use for yourself little, but give to others much."

- Albert Einstein

"If I am not for myself who is for me? And when I am for myself what am I? And if not now, when?"

- Hillel

CHAPTER TWENTY-FIVE
THE BIBLE AND
HOMOSEXUALITY

Surprise: The Bible does not oppose homosexual activity

The prevailing thought about the Bible is that it is against homosexuality, and any gay or lesbian person who believes in God and the Bible struggles with this perception.

This essay will show that the Bible is not opposed to homosexuals and homosexual acts. These are the facts:

1) The Bible does not have laws against lesbianism. There is a law about not having sex during a woman's monthly period as stated in Leviticus 18:19. Furthermore, Leviticus 18:23 states: *A woman must not present herself to an animal to have sexual relations with it: that is perversion.* And that is as much as is said about "aberrant" sexual behavior as it pertains to women.

2) In Leviticus 18:22, the Bible does prohibit sexual acts between men: *Do not lie with a man as one lies with a woman. That is detestable.*

Let us try to understand this law. First let's examine the relationship between King David and Jonathan, King Saul's son. When Jonathan died in battle, King David wrote a poem lamenting his demise. In Samuel: 1:25, he wrote: *"I grieve for you, Jonathan my brother: You were very dear to me. Your love for me was wonderful. More wonderful than that of women."*

This poem reveals that King David and Jonathan had a loving relationship, which they felt was even more wonderful than a loving relationship with a woman.

Evolution by God

The Bible has tremendous respect for King David. He is one of the most cherished of Bible heroes. Yet he was never criticized for having an intimate relationship with Jonathan. How can the Bible approve of this relationship in spite of the law in Leviticus 18:22, unless the relationship between the two men was assumed to be platonic?

In order to explain this let's look at another episode:

In Genesis 24:1-4 it is written: *Abraham was now old and well advanced in years and the Lord had blessed him in every way. He said to his chief servant in his household "Put your hand under my thigh. I want you to swear by the Lord, that you will not get a wife for my son from the daughters of the Canaanites among whom I am living, but will go to my country and my own relatives and get a wife for my son Isaac."*

In this episode Abraham asks his servant to solemnly swear on an extremely important matter, and, to make this a binding holy contract, he asked him to put his hand under Abraham's thigh, in order to hold Abraham's testicles and penis. Why? According to the Talmud, the penis was a sacred organ. The contract or covenant between God and Israel was sealed by the circumcision of every man and child. The penis had the signature of this covenant.

In modern society, the sexual organs are looked upon negatively—to be hidden from view, and untouchable in public. Not so in biblical times. The penises and testicles were considered sacred because they are the source for propagating mankind. *Be fruitful and multiply,* the Bible decrees. As you can see, one man can hold the sexual organs of another without feeling strange about it.

Now let's look to another story. When God decided to destroy Sodom and Gomorrah and save Lot's life, He sent two angels to Lot to escort him out of Sodom. In Genesis 19:1 it is written: *Before they had gone to bed, all the men from every part of the city of Sodom—both young and old surrounded the house. They called to Lot: "Where are the men who came to you tonight? Bring them out to us so we can have sex with them."*

As you see, the Sodomites were violent and wanted to rape these angels (who appeared as human males). A Sodomite act is defined as having anal sex.

From the above stories we can conclude that the Bible is not opposed to homosexual relationships in general. Women can have sex with other women without any limitation. Men can do the same, but with one exception: Anal sex. Why? *Because the penis is sacred!* However, a condom isolates the penis from the anal canal, and protects it against disease. Therefore, it may be possible (and even permissible) to have anal sex without defiling the penis. Assuming my theory is correct, now, with the condom in use, gay men would still be able to adhere to their religious principles and not worry about contracting a sexual disease. A win-win solution.

I assume that many readers will feel uncomfortable with my solution to the issue of anal sex within the homosexual community. However, it would be difficult to disagree with the wisdom of regularly using a condom as a means of protection against sex-related disease.

As I have stated in previous articles, we have seen demonstrated that God is limited in His ability to create a perfect world and that in Exodus 3:14, He even admits to His own imperfection. Manifestation of this is seen in the earth that God created and on which He frequently imposes such "natural" disasters as: earthquakes, tsunamis, floods, tornadoes, and droughts. Such powerful calamities as these invariably kill, maim, or displace thousands of people annually across the globe. Also, in His image God created the human race as imperfect, and therefore subject to such negative traits as: hatred, envy, and greed—invariably at the root of chaos, holocaust, and war.

The same concept holds true for the 3.5% (results of a 2013 Gallup poll) of our U.S. population that identifies as gay, lesbian, or bisexual. Here is another example of imperfection within a system created by God, whose primary purpose, we have come to believe, is procreation of the species. In spite of the fact that homosexuality does not fulfill this intended purpose, the human race has nonetheless continued to flourish, and even grown exponentially. Considering that fact, and that homosexuality is a long-established state of being within our normally acceptable parameters, we can only make the best of the situation, as it not about to change. My plan describes how to accomplish it. *

* Recently, in a 5-4 vote, the Supreme Court of the United States ruled unconstitutional a 1996 law that denies federal benefits to same-sex couples. By declining to decide a related case in California, they left it open for recognition of same-sex marriage in that state, despite the hotly contested Proposition 8 that lost in a statewide election. While this ruling does not provide a nationwide mandate on the issue, the new ruling, should it be deemed legal in the State of California, would increase the number of states allowing gay marriage to thirteen. This turn of the tide toward acceptance of what is still considered by many an aberrant or alternative lifestyle, moves it increasingly closer to legitimacy and to all the rights, privileges, and respect that classification provides. As the human race continues to evolve in the 21st century, it is realizing increasingly that homosexuality is merely one more variation out of multitudes that have come to define our imperfect human race.

Ultimately, gay and lesbian couples are no different from anyone else in their dreams and desires for love and family. They are human, after all. In legalized marriage, they seek only equality under the law, a major departure from the strict canons of the Holy Bible, as dictated during the Bronze Age of 3,000 years ago. This is not to give the impression that their battle for equality has already been won. Merely that as the general population is increasingly educated and enlightened their perception of normalcy expands accordingly. Those religious tenets that have long dictated their thinking do not have to be denied as much as they would do well to be updated. The Oral Law provides for such evolutionary thinking. The intractable Bible, unfortunately, cannot. ✿

CHAPTER TWENTY-SIX
STANDING YOUR GROUND

"if someone is coming to kill you, rise early and kill him."

- Talmud, Sanhedrin 72a

Since the controversial trial in which a Florida neighborhood watch volunteer fatally shot a 17-year old African-American during a physical altercation, there has been much hue and cry over the jury verdict of acquittal, primarily along racial lines. Although it has been stated repeatedly that none of the evidence in the case supported the claim of racial bias, the mainstream media and a number of prominent activists immediately took that position. In short order, they demanded a federal investigation as well as the repeal of Florida's Stand Your Ground law, which Governor Rick Scott refused to do. The same was asked of all states with Stand Your Ground or No Duty to Retreat laws, which essentially sanction the use of deadly force as a means of self preservation.

Besides charging defendant George Zimmerman with racial profiling the unarmed Trayvon Martin, accusatory fingers pointed toward their traditional political foes. On top of the list they placed the National Rifle Association for their position in support of the right to bear arms. Such laws naturally gained greater traction in the wake of 9/11. However, they are not unrelated to the Second Amendment of our US Constitution's Bill of Rights, which was based, in part, on the earlier Castle Doctrine of English common law. And hasn't the civilized world always deemed some version of self defense or "stand your ground" as a natural human right? Aside from its passage into English law in

by Michael Bash

the 17th century and American jurisprudence in the 18th, the Bible made its similar position clear 3,000 years earlier. As such, all these policies have contributed a fundamental building block to the enduringly moral foundation of Western civilization.

According to Exodus 22:2, "If a thief is discovered breaking into one's home, and is subsequently killed while doing so, the one who kills him bears no guilt for having done so." This position is reinforced by a widely quoted rabbinic statement from the Torah: "If someone comes to kill you, get up and kill him." There are numerous versions of this perspective woven throughout the fabric of Judaic law, but they vary in terms of interpretation and circumstance. Basically, they all approve the right to defend one's life and home against an intruder rather than be forced to retreat.

In 2009 Rabbi Yirmiyahu Ullman (www.rabbiullman. com) responded to an inquiry on the issue of self-defense against terrorism. He stated that although Jews would rather have peace than war, the Torah teaches them the need to fight and win. He offered several examples of this from religious text, including one that sanctions preemptive action. In Sanhedrin 72a, the Talmud teaches a variation of the above-quoted passage from Exodus: "If someone comes to kill you, arise and kill him first." Affirming this principle, the Shulchan Aruch (Choshen Mishpat 125:1) states, "If one sees that someone is pursuing him with the intention to kill him, he is permitted to defend himself and take the life of he who is pursuing him."

In Exodus 14:13-14, Moses tells his people who are fleeing from Pharaoh, "Do not fear! Stand your ground and see the victory the LORD will win for you today. For these Egyptians whom you see today you will never see again. The LORD will fight for you; you have only to keep still."

In Ephesians 6:14, the New Testament puts forth its

own spin on this issue, as follows: "Therefore put on the full armor of God, so that when the day of evil comes, you may be able to stand your ground, and after you have done everything, to stand."

Intentionally denying an innocent individual the right to life is justifiably punishable in the eyes of the law, but to deny one the right to defend himself against someone who would do him harm has no rational support in the eyes of man or of God.

As we evolve in this universe along with God, there remains the necessity to evolve our codes of behavior. In that respect, the basic instinct to prevail in a principled manner has been largely responsible for man's ability to adapt to his environment for the past two-and-a-half million years. Not only have the fittest of us survived over time, but also those with a strong regard for human life and dignity. The endless struggle to live while supported by an ethical set of laws has always been the natural order of things, and ultimately distinguishes civilized man from his barbarian counterparts.

Author Michael Bash is evolving... He is also reinventing... repurposing... and rezoning.

A word from Mr. Bash:

In my first book, I shared insights and observations from my spiritual and scientific perspectives. My forthcoming book, *The Rezoning*, reveals the novel strategies and tactics I have used over the past half-century that I credit for my consistent success as a businessperson and human being.

Applied to the real estate industry, a permit to rezone allows for the reclassification of a property or neighborhood, causing it to become subject to a more accommodating set of rules and restrictions. In my profession, it has allowed me to repurpose, for example, a one-acre property that had previously been restricted to a single family home for the development of twenty apartment units on that same piece of land. Taking this one simple action automatically increased the worth of the property ten times over—by a full 1,000%. In this manner, acreage worth $100,000 under one zoning ordinance would enjoy an elevated value of $1 million the moment of its approval for multiple units under a different ordinance.

I use the following example to illustrate the simplicity with which rezoning works: Imagine you just bought a new Cadillac automobile for $80,000. I come to visit you, and with a wave of my magic wand, I instantly transform your Cadillac into a brand new Bentley worth $200,000. Such is the incredible power of rezoning, and its ability to almost instantly reap massive profits.

The first time I encountered this phenomenon was in 1963 at age 32, when I parlayed a mere $1,500 into a million-dollar profit—my first of quite a few more to come. Bear in mind that 1963 was half a century ago, and that $1 million at that time was the equivalent of approximately $15 million in today's deflated currency.

Chapter One of *The Rezoning* describes how I made that first million dollars using this process. Over the subsequent decades, I became increasingly proficient in the procedure, and began applying it to every aspect of my life—business opportunities as well as personal and social. As a result, I have strengthened my physical and emotional health, enriched all my relationships, lived a balanced, fulfilling existence, and along the way achieved an enduring peace of mind.

I even rezoned my long-term marriage from that of an average couple with normal expectations to a rare union in which we both enjoyed an enormous measure of love and happiness within the comfort and security of a luxurious and abundant lifestyle.

In Chapter Two, I offer an example of how I have utilized the rezoning process outside the field of real estate. In 1979, I met media mogul Rupert Murdock by chance in the elevator of a Manhattan office building, and within an hour I had negotiated the purchase of his failing magazine publication and written him a check for $100,000. With that relatively small investment I quickly managed to turn the enterprise, into which Murdock had already sunk and lost $12 million, into a profitable business.

To illustrate the power of my rezoning skills, I provide numerous fact-based examples of opportunities that came my way—how I managed to recognize their huge potential and then maximize it in every conceivable way. Along with my various real estate ventures and marriage, I have rezoned such varied entities as a mountain, a castle, milk cows, magazines, a disaffected rich kid, and my current wholly satisfying personal relationship—which has been a rezoning of a mutual kind.

Look for the release of *The Rezoning* in early 2014. Once you have read it all the way through, you will be ready to apply the techniques I describe. Then there is nothing to stop you from rezoning your own life accordingly, and ultimately living it on a level you previously only dreamed possible.

Evolve... Reinvent...Repurpose...*Rezone.*

MichaelBash

www.evolutionbygod.com

ABOUT THE AUTHOR

Michael Bash

Rooted in equal parts science and religion, the author holds a unique perspective on the unremitting clash between Darwinism and Creationism.

Born and raised in Jerusalem, Michael Bash developed a strong interest as a youth in religious theory and studied the Bible, the Talmud and Rashi.

Over the years, Michael continued his passion, and his studies included Creationism, Intelligent Design, along with various other Christian-oriented perspectives.

Currently, Mr. Bash is writing new articles for his website at: www.evolutionbygod.com, in which he plans to expand on how specific applications of science and technology provide rational explanation for the possible existence of a personal God, one that is capable of answering millions of prayers simultaneously. The question about how prayers may be answered has baffled even the most dedicated of religious scholars for thousands of years!

CPSIA information can be obtained at www.ICGtesting.com
Printed in the USA
LVOW06s1459030314

375743LV00040B/1536/P

9 781936 525959